Understanding Applied
Behavior Analysis

of related interest

Tales from the Table
Lovaas/ABA Intervention with Children on the Autistic Spectrum
Margaret Anderson
ISBN 978 1 84310 306 6

Video Modelling and Behaviour Analysis
A Guide for Teaching Social Skills to Children with Autism
Christos Nikopoulos and Mickey Keenan
Foreword by Sandy Hobbs
ISBN 9781843103387

Applied Behaviour Analysis and Autism
Building A Future Together
Edited by Mickey Keenan, Mary Henderson, Ken P. Kerr and Karola Dillenburger
Foreword by Professor Gina Green
ISBN 978 1 84310 310 3

Parents' Education as Autism Therapists
Applied Behaviour Analysis in Context
Edited by Mickey Keenan, Ken P. Kerr and Karola Dillenburger
Foreword by Bobby Newman
ISBN 978 1 85302 778 9

Replays
Using Play to Enhance Emotional and Behavioral Development for Children with Autism Spectrum Disorders
Karen Levine and Naomi Chedd
ISBN 978 1 84310 832 0

The Verbal Behavior Approach
How to Teach Children with Autism and Related Disorders
Mary Lynch Barbera
With Tracy Rasmussen
Foreword by Mark L. Sundberg, PhD, BCBA
ISBN 978 1 84310 852 8

The Miller Method ®
Developing the Capacities of Children on the Autism Spectrum
Arnold Miller
With Kristina Chrétien
ISBN 978 1 84310 722 4

Achieving Best Behavior for Children with Developmental Disabilities
A Step-By-Step Workbook for Parents and Carers
Pamela Lewis
ISBN 978 1 84310 809 2

Encouraging Appropriate Behavior for Children on the Autism Spectrum
Frequently Asked Questions
Shira Richman
ISBN 978 1 84310 825 2

Understanding Applied Behavior Analysis

An Introduction to ABA for Parents, Teachers, and other Professionals

Albert J. Kearney

Jessica Kingsley Publishers
London and Philadelphia

First published in 2008
by Jessica Kingsley Publishers
116 Pentonville Road
London N1 9JB, UK
and
400 Market Street, Suite 400
Philadelphia, PA 19106, USA

www.jkp.com

Library of Congress Cataloging in Publication Data
A CIP catalog record for this book is available from the Library of Congress

British Library Cataloguing in Publication Data
A CIP catalogue record for this book is available from the British Library

ISBN 978 1 84310 860 3

Printed and bound in the United States by
Thomson-Shore, Inc.

*To Joe Cautela (1927–1999), my teacher,
mentor and friend, for helping me to understand ABA,
a long time ago.*

ACKNOWLEDGMENTS

One of the problems with writing acknowledgments is the fear of leaving someone out. Right now I feel like I could double the size of this whole book if I mentioned the names of everyone who has helped me learn about applied behavior analysis (ABA), assisted in the production of this book, or contributed in some other major way to this work.

There are, however, certain people whom I absolutely, positively must thank. I should begin by thanking the three people who taught me about ABA back in my student days, Joe Cautela, Al Jurgela and Bruce Baker, and the person who gave me my first opportunity to apply behavior analysis professionally, Mike Fabien, the first Director of Pupil Services for the Maynard Public Schools.

During the writing of this book several old friends and relatives who have various professional involvements with ABA have read various "editions" of the manuscript and made countless helpful suggestions as it evolved. These include Liz Crowley, reading specialist of the Whitman-Hanson Regional School District; Shelley Green, program specialist of the Concord Area Special Education Collaborative; Jeanne Kearney, fourth-grade teacher (and former ABA paraprofessional) of the Bellingham Public Schools; Judy Robinson, inclusion coordinator of the Medfield Public Schools; Meg Robinson, case manager at the New England Center for Children; and John Sforza, special education teacher (and former special education director) of the Maynard Public Schools. Thanks also to my new friends at Jessica Kingsley Publishers, Steve Jones, Melanie Wilson, and Lucy Mitchell, for all their help and patience.

Last but certainly not least, special thanks to the other Dr. Kearney, my wife Anne of the South Shore Mental Health Center and Action Therapies, who has been with me through just about all of this and has contributed greatly at every step of the way.

CONTENTS

Part 1: The ABCs of ABA

Part 2: Putting It All Together

INTRODUCTION

There are countless scholarly texts and precise scientific volumes that have been written about applied behavior analysis (ABA). This is not one of them. *Understanding Applied Behavior Analysis* is written especially to help introduce applied behavior analysis to parents of children involved in ABA-based programs, teachers and administrators whose classrooms and schools are serving an increasing number of students receiving ABA-based interventions, paraprofessionals working directly on the front lines with these children, and anyone else working under the guidance of ABA specialists. *Understanding Applied Behavior Analysis* is intended to accomplish this by providing a brief introduction to basic terminology, underlying principles, and commonly used ABA treatment procedures.

Probably the first term that many readers find themselves mystified by is the term *applied behavior analysis* itself. While you'll certainly get a more thorough understanding of ABA as you read through this book, just to help you get started you should know that applied behavior analysis is an approach to changing behaviors that uses procedures based on scientifically established principles of learning. In ABA the behaviors targeted for change are behaviors that are usually socially important to someone in some way. As a scientific approach to behavior change, ABA involves a considerable amount of monitoring of the intervention programs, collecting data about the behaviors that we hope to change, and ongoing evaluation of the effectiveness of the intervention procedures.

Most fields of science develop extensive and often confusing vocabularies of their own over the years and ABA is no exception. ABA language can be particularly intimidating to people new to ABA. Educators have often complained about the intimidating terminology used by some of the experts who have provided ABA training programs for them. A main goal of this book is to demystify the esoteric jargon commonly used in the ABA world. I hope to give readers a running start by providing an understanding of what the experts are talking and writing about before they get confused, frustrated and turned off by it all, which has too often been the case in the past.

Understanding Applied Behavior Analysis presents the basics, or the ABCs, of ABA. While ABA is the abbreviation for applied behavior analysis, as far as this book is concerned the letters ABC have a double meaning. The use of ABCs is of course intended to let readers know that this is an ABA primer, written for those who have little or no background in ABA. But as the more ABA-savvy reader will know, ABC also stands for the three building blocks upon which ABA is based, the building blocks that B. F. Skinner referred to as the contingencies of reinforcement—the antecedents, behaviors, and consequences. This book provides a solid introduction to these and other behavior analytic terms and concepts.

Besides being an introduction to ABA, *Understanding Applied Behavior Analysis* is also a user-friendly translation of professional jargon into *plain English*, sort of like an ABA to plain English dictionary. Rather than providing formal definitions of terms, I try to provide explanations of ABA terms and concepts in everyday common-sense language. So you should acquire a pretty good understanding of basic ABA vocabulary along the way.

I'll take you through all this as painlessly as I can. I've attempted to include occasional humor to help reduce the anxiety that some readers may experience when first exposed to behavior analytic language and literature. Although the writing style is intentionally light, the content is as accurate as you'll find in those graduate-level textbooks. While reading this book alone won't make you an expert practitioner of ABA, I hope it will make you an informed consumer or knowledgeable observer, sort of like being a knowledgeable baseball fan.

In Part 1, "The ABCs of ABA," I'll first explain what ABA is in more detail and talk about those basic principles or building blocks of ABA—antecedents, behaviors, and consequences. Building on this beginning, the various learning operations and reinforcement schedules of operant conditioning will then be presented. Other kinds of learning are also briefly introduced. In Part 2, "Putting It All Together," we'll talk more about practical applications of these basic principles as we discuss how the science of behavior analysis can be applied to real life everyday behavior problems. A systematic approach to behavioral assessment will be presented and many of the more common behavioral intervention techniques that have been employed with children will be described. Behavior analysts can be very creative and new applications seem to be appearing all the time. Although the presentation of ABA techniques can of course not be complete, we'll certainly present the key techniques you are likely to encounter.

I've tried to use numerous examples to illustrate many of the concepts presented. But examples can get boring, especially when certain words like *they*, *the student*, *the child*, and so forth just repeat themselves over and over again. So I chose a couple of fictional friends, whom some readers may remember, to play the parts of the children (and occasionally adults) in the examples used to help bring various points to life.

Understanding Applied Behavior Analysis can be used in a variety of ways. It is designed to be read cover to cover as well as being usable as a nonalphabetical glossary. The terms and concepts included build on each other throughout the text to provide a more complete understanding than one might acquire by simply looking up words here and there. Rather than presenting terms in alphabetical order, they are introduced in logical order so that by becoming familiar with certain basic terms first it should be easier to understand some of the other terms when you run into them later in the book. The quick reference A–Z, along with the table of contents, is placed at the front of the book.

After reading through the book, just stick it on a nearby bookshelf to keep it handy as a quick and easy reference book or as a companion to more specialized texts. As one reader suggested, you can think of your *Understanding Applied Behavior Analysis* as your Swiss army knife of ABA books!

This book has been many years in the making and countless people have contributed to its development over the years. If you have any comments or suggestions for the second edition, or perhaps have a good real-life example of any of the concepts presented, by all means send them on in to me, care of Jessica Kingsley Publishers.

So now if there are any terms that you were wondering about you can just turn to the quick reference A–Z that begins on the next page to see where to find those terms. Or you can turn to Chapter 1 and start at the beginning. Either way. The explanations you'll find are a good first step in understanding ABA, sort of like a step in the shaping process. What's that you say? You don't know what shaping is? Well, I could come right out and tell you, but you're much more likely to remember if you look it up yourself. So now read on, or if you're one of those people who like to read the end of mysteries first, you can just turn to page 73 to find *shaping*.

QUICK REFERENCE A–Z

Part 1

THE ABCs OF ABA

Chapter 1

WHAT DOES ABA MEAN?

All of a sudden in the last few years we seem to be hearing the term ABA whenever anyone talks about children with autistic spectrum disorders (ASDs). Especially if we are parents, teachers, or have another role in schools these days, we are often given the impression that ABA is the only thing that's going to save these children, and we'd better do it, and do it right now, or else we are in big trouble. Sounds pretty intimidating, doesn't it?

You may be wondering what the heck is ABA anyway? Where did it come from? And how am I supposed to "do" ABA when I know next to nothing about this stuff? Where can I get some answers?

Well, you've come to the right place, at least to get a good start. We're going to go over the ABCs of ABA so you'll have a better idea about what behavioral psychologists, behaviorologists, special educators and behavior analysts are doing to your children and students, and you'll be better able to help when these kids are at home or integrated into your classroom. But first, a brief background check on ABA, because you may already know more about ABA than you think you do.

ABA, applied behavior analysis   ABA is the abbreviation for *applied behavior analysis.* As I mentioned in the Introduction, ABA is an approach to changing socially useful behaviors that employs scientifically established principles of learning to bring about these changes. At first glance it might appear that ABA is simply the practice of using incentives to reward "good" behavior while ignoring "bad" behavior. Actually, there's more to ABA, a lot more, and you're going to learn a lot more about ABA as you read through this book. From the beginning, though, you should be aware of three important characteristics of ABA that will help explain just what ABA "is." First, the behaviors we target for change are behaviors that can have real-life applications for the person we are working with. That's the applied part. Second, we are working with real, observable measurable behaviors rather than some abstract diagnosis, and, as we will soon see, the procedures used in ABA are based on scientifically established principles of learning. That's where behavior comes in. The third critical characteristic of ABA is that decisions in ABA are made based on objective data that is collected to help understand what effect, if any, the interventions being used are actually having on the behavior. In many ways ABA is like an ongoing experiment in that we keep close watch over what's happening as a result of our interventions and quickly make adjustments as needed. That's the analysis part.

In using behavioral approaches it is of course very important that we pay close attention to the behaviors that we want to change. But it is also quite important that we pay attention to other factors as well, especially what immediately precedes or happens before the behavior, sometimes called the *Antecedents*, and the events which follow the *Behaviors*, sometimes called the *Consequences*. These three factors—the As, the Bs, and the Cs of behavior and what they have to do with ABA—are the main topics of the first part of this book.

Contingency of reinforcement The As, Bs and Cs are so closely related that Skinner used a special term when talking about them, *contingency of reinforcement*, which is a three-part concept: "(1) an occasion upon which behavior occurs, (2) the behavior itself, and (3) the consequences of the behavior" (Skinner 1968, p. 4).

Contrary to popular belief, ABA is not new. The Association for Behavior Analysis International, which started out in the United States as the Midwest Association for Behavior Analysis, has been around since 1974. The *Journal of Applied Behavior Analysis* was first published in 1968, so obviously the field of ABA has been around even longer. There is often some debate about who was the first to use this term or that term. While there is a lot of debate over who came up with the term *behavior therapy* I haven't heard much debate about who first used the term applied behavior analysis. No one seems to know for sure anyway. Some think Ullman and Krasner were the first to use ABA in their 1965 book *Case Studies in Behavior Modification*. Others say it is likely that ABA was first used by Montrose Wolf, one of the founders and the first editor of the *Journal of Applied Behavior Analysis* (usually just called JABA). Wolf may be best known for his use of ABA principles in remedial education programs for children known as The Juniper Gardens Children's Project, located in Kansas City, Kansas.

Applied behavior analysis is based on the work of the great American psychologist B. F. Skinner. Many of Skinner's scientific contributions had to do with studying behavior and the process of learning in psychology laboratories. Skinner and his students often studied the behavior of animals such as rats and pigeons and analyzed their behavior under closely monitored conditions. Skinner's work, which is sometimes referred to as *behavior analysis* or the *experimental analysis of behavior*, has also been applied successfully to humans in numerous ways. ABA takes the findings of Skinner and his followers and applies these findings to human beings in a variety of settings such as schools, hospitals, work places, casinos, sports, and homes. The *Association for Behavior Analysis International* now has more than 20 special interest groups for its members, representing such varied areas of interest and application of ABA principles as autism, behavioral gerontology, behaviorists for social action, organizational behavior management and clinical behavior analysis. While we'll get into greater detail later, the ABA approach combines interventions usually based on a particular kind of learning commonly associated with Skinner (i.e. operant conditioning) with methods for ongoing objective monitoring of whether or not a particular intervention (or treatment) is working.

What's in a name?

People working in ABA use a lot of different titles to describe themselves. Here are a few of the more common titles, in case you were wondering who these guys are anyway.

Behavior analyst A *behavior analyst* is someone who does applied behavior analysis, and who, it is hoped, is properly trained to do it well. Although way back in the twentieth century behavior analysts were mostly psychologists or educators who had specialized training and experience in ABA, in recent years there are increasing numbers of undergraduate and graduate programs specifically in ABA. So these days someone called a behavior analyst may or may not have significant training in other areas of psychology or another related field as well.

BCBA A *BCBA* is a *board-certified behavior analyst*. That is, a behavior analyst who has met considerable educational requirements and passed a test to demonstrate their knowledge of ABA. Again, while the training of BCBAs may be limited to ABA, they may also be trained as psychologists, special educators, or be professionals in other disciplines.

Behavior therapy, behavior therapist A *behavior therapist* is someone who does behavior therapy, and, like a behavior analyst, should be trained to do it well. *Behavior therapy* is generally thought of as an approach to psychotherapy that relies on the use of therapeutic techniques based on principles of learning, primarily operant and classical conditioning. Behavior therapy typically involves therapy sessions with a behavior therapist, often a specially trained psychologist, but sometimes psychiatrists, social workers, nurses, counselors or others. Much of the treatment in behavior therapy involves guided talking with cooperative clients, who may be children or adults, about their problems and the directed use of behavior therapy techniques, many of which are ABA based.

Perhaps the best-known behavior therapy technique is systematic desensitization, originally developed by Joseph Wolpe (1958) and demonstrated to be particularly effective in treating phobias.

Cognitive behavior therapy, cognitive behavior therapist   *Cognitive behavior therapy* refers to any of a number of types of psychotherapy that emphasize trying to help clients deal better with their problems by helping them to change the ways they think or talk to themselves about things. There are many different approaches to cognitive behavior therapy that vary in how much they rely on principles of learning. One problem area that cognitive behavior therapy seems to be particularly helpful for is in treating depression. While cognitive behavior therapy isn't generally considered to be part of ABA, many cognitive behavior therapists use ABA principles in their work.

Behaviorology, behaviorologist   Although there are some pretty lengthy and complicated definitions of behaviorology out there, a simplified description might be something like, *behaviorology* is "the science of contingent relations between behavior and other events." Behaviorology is a newer term than ABA. It first appeared in the 1980s, to describe the emerging scientific approach to the study of behavior that continues to evolve from psychology and other disciplines. Behaviorology is broader than we generally think of ABA, is becoming a field of its own, and is likely to become more widely known as time goes on. While many behaviorologists belong to the *Association for Behavior Analysis International*, there is another professional organization for *behaviorologists* called *The International Society for Behaviorology*.

Now that you have a general idea of what ABA is all about, it's time to get an even better understanding of ABA. I'd like to start all this with a section on antecedents, since it seems like it would be a lot neater to go alphabetically, A, B, C. But it really will help more with a better understanding of A, or antecedents, if we do B, or behavior, first, so here we go…

Chapter 2

WHAT IS BEHAVIOR?

Behavior   *Behavior* is a word we hear and use quite a bit. Most of us take it for granted that we know what it means when we hear or see the word behavior. According to one definition in Webster's dictionary, behavior is "the manner of conducting oneself." That's fine, but isn't that just a fancy way of saying, "The way we act?"

Another more formal definition by a behavioral psychologist would be something like: *behavior is any external or internal observable and measurable act of an organism.* That sounds complicated, but when we take this definition apart piece by piece it starts to make more sense. Once again, I'd rather start at the beginning and work through this definition in a nice, orderly, step-by-step fashion, but for some reason it makes more sense to start at the end and work toward the front. How do I keep getting myself into these things?

Psychologists work with lots of different living creatures, humans of course, but also monkeys, pigeons, rats, dolphins, and dogs, among others. So to be inclusive we often use the fancy word *organism*. But as far as we are concerned, for our purposes in this book, we're talking about human beings, people, persons! By an *act* we aren't talking about part of a play or a comedy routine, but an action, something somebody actually *does*. It could be walking, talking, or kicking a soccer ball. It could be writing the letters of the alphabet, making eye contact with a teacher, or singing a song. These acts can clearly be observed (seen, heard, etc.) and measured (e.g. counted) in a variety of ways that we will talk about later. But they really do have to be objective acts, not just a subjective personal opinion or descriptive labels (such as saying someone is aggressive, depressed, or anxious and the like) inferred from seemingly related acts.

Those labels aren't really observable acts, are they? They are all adjectives used to describe objective acts or behaviors. What gets called an aggressive act might be anything from giving someone a dirty look to shooting them with a gun. So if we just say "aggressive" without specifying the act, we really don't know what the speaker observed or what the culprit really did, and we can easily mislead someone else or be misled ourselves.

Dead Man Rule   Some people find it helpful to think of a behavior as being some kind of movement. Thinking of behavior as movement means that sitting still and keeping quiet are not behaviors. There is an old saying by Ogden Lindsley, one of the pioneers of precision teaching, called the *Dead Man Rule*. "If a dead man can do it, it's not a behavior." So if you're not sure if something is a behavior or not, just ask yourself whether or not a dead man can do it. Using the Dead Man Rule at least helps narrow down some of the possibilities.

When we say the act can be either external or internal, we're talking about the person's body, that is, the person who performs the act or behavior. External acts are things that occur outside the body that most anyone around could directly observe and recognize. These external acts are often described as overt or public behaviors. Brushing your teeth, doing a dance, talking on the telephone are overt behaviors. But we also have internal, covert, private behaviors. These internal, covert behaviors include physiological acts of our bodies, such as the beating of our hearts and the digestion going on in our stomachs. Even emitting brain waves are internal behaviors that are not so easily or directly observed. Usually medical instruments of some kind or other are needed to observe and measure covert physiological behaviors, but just because no one sees the actions of these internal bodily organs directly doesn't mean that they are not behaviors.

Other internal, covert or private behaviors are actions or events that we commonly think of not as physiological behaviors but rather as *psychological* behaviors. These include behaviors such as thinking and having images and feelings. Pretty much the only observer of these actions is the person doing or experiencing them, so they can be awfully hard to work with. But when you stop and think about it, we usually know what we're thinking about ourselves, whether we're just talking to ourselves "quietly inside our heads," or thinking in images or pictures. After all, don't we often tell others what we're thinking and describe what we are imagining when we want to? The same goes for feelings. While sometimes our facial expressions and other external actions give away how we are feeling, we generally know what feelings we are experiencing, even if we choose to outwardly act differently in hopes of hiding our feelings from others. So external acts and internal acts, both physiological and psychological acts, are all types of behavior. Just about everything you and your body do can be considered behavior. To paraphrase Skinner, skin is not a boundary to behavior. Recognizing internal behavior as well as external behavior is often referred to as *radical behaviorism*.

Frequency and **rate** So to complete our definition of behavior, how do we *measure* an act? Well, there are a variety of ways. The simplest is just to count how many times a particular behavior occurs. We call this count of a behavior its *frequency*. But the frequency alone usually isn't very helpful. Suppose we say a baseball player got two hits. At first that might seem pretty good if we assume we're talking about just one game, but we really haven't said yet how many times at bat the player had. What if those two hits were for a whole season? Not so good. So the number of behaviors must be put into a meaningful context so that it makes sense, such as the number of opportunities or length of time. This context gives us a more useful measure than frequency alone, which we call the *rate* of behavior. For baseball players we calculate their batting average by dividing the number of hits by the number of times at bat. (Well, sort of. We don't count bases on balls and... Oh, never mind, you get the idea.) We will talk more about ways to observe and measure behaviors later. So finally we can simply say that behavior is anything a living person does outside or inside their body that can be observed and counted in some way.

Learning Most human behavior is the result of one or more of three factors usually acting together. These three factors are:

1. our heredity or genetic endowment

2. physiological changes that happen to us after conception (such as maturation and the effects of disease and accidents), and

3. behavior-changing experiences that we call *learning*.

Numerous books have been written about the seemingly countless theories of learning that scholars have proposed. Those definitions that include an objective, scientific study of learning can mostly be boiled down to a more practical definition of learning as *any relatively permanent change in behavior that results from interaction with the environment.*

When we hear the word *environment* we usually think of trees, rivers, meadows, oceans, and other parts of our natural environment. These are certainly important, but when we're talking about behavior, other parts of our physical and social environment are important too. Human-made objects such as tools, books, computers and TV sets, as well as the other people around us and their behavior, are all parts of our environment and can influence our behavior.

Using genetic engineering to change our behavior by changing our genetic makeup is far from being practical, and bringing about other physical changes through medical treatments such as drugs does not have reliable and specific results, is not always reversible, and risks side effects. So this leaves learning as our last and best chance to change behavior. Of these three factors, learning is the one we can do the most about. But most of the time the learning that we do is unplanned, somewhat random, and not very efficient. Since learning takes place through interaction with the environment, learning and therefore behavior can best be modified through planned changes of the environment and learning process.

Environments   Now that I've mentioned the environment and that it has a lot to do with behavior, I guess I should explain more about what I mean by *environment*. Sometimes we hear people talking about different kinds of environments. Here are some names for environments I bet you don't hear everyday.

Natural environment   When most of us hear the *natural environment* mentioned we first think about the great outdoors. But natural environment can have another meaning. When we put our behaviorist hats on, we start thinking more about social environments. When we're thinking about social environments, the natural environment pretty much means what we often call the *real world*, where most of us spend most of our time. For children, part of the natural environment would be mainstream classrooms, without any special accommodations, modifications, or specialized instruction. While there certainly are factors operating in the natural environment that will influence their behavior, they are the same things that just about everyone else is exposed to. The natural environment does a pretty good job of socializing most people, but sometimes things can get a bit wild in the natural environment and end up shaping all sorts of maladaptive anti-social and dysfunctional behaviors.

Prosthetic environment   A *prosthetic environment* is an environment that helps an individual to behave more like his or her typical peers. Just as a prosthetic device such as an artificial limb or hearing aid may help "level the playing field" as some might say, a prosthetic environment may be a very highly structured arrangement, perhaps with lots of help built in to encourage the individual to behave more adaptively and appropriately. A prosthetic environment helps teach and/or maintain a particular pattern of behavior that the child would not currently perform dependably in the natural environment. Perhaps Dick doesn't perform the behavior in the natural environment because he hasn't learned the skill yet, or perhaps because there is no reason or motivation for him the way the natural environment is currently set up. If Dick has attention deficit hyperactivity disorder (ADHD), for example, he might more easily pay attention to his teacher in a classroom that does not have a lot of novel stimulation. If Dick has a habit of looking out of the window to watch another class at recess, and maybe starts daydreaming about being out there too, perhaps drawing the window shades during recess time would help minimize distractions. On the other hand, a lot of rapid changes in stimuli, if well planned, may help Dick focus better on the task at hand, like when he amazes everyone when he gets so absorbed by his fast-paced video games.

Therapeutic environment   A *therapeutic environment* is an environment that is intended to help the student to eventually become more independent of it and to be able to behave more like typical peers when in the natural environment. Sometimes a student with serious behavioral problems needs to be placed in a specialized self-contained classroom, for everyone's good. Intense treatment while placed in that specialized environment should make it possible for Dick to acquire the behavioral patterns he needs to learn to be eventually integrated back into the mainstream classroom and to succeed in the natural environment.

Although we might be able to make a pretty good guess, we don't really know for sure if an environment is prosthetic or therapeutic until the situation is *naturalized* again, and we can see if the new behavior continues appropriately or not. If the new behavior continues in the natural environment, then the prior situation functioned as a therapeutic environment. If the new behavior stops in the natural environment, then the prior situation functioned as a prosthetic environment. So sometimes the same environment may be prosthetic and at other times it may be therapeutic. We can't tell for sure just by looking at how the environment is structured or arranged; we really have to see what effect it has on behavior. Also, the same environment at the same time can be prosthetic for one behavior and therapeutic for another. Again, it depends on the effect the environment is having on each behavior.

Behavior modification   Although ABA is a term that may be new to many of us, people who worked in public education during the second half of the twentieth century are likely to be more familiar with the term *behavior modification*. Behavior modification, sometimes referred to as Behavior Mod, has been defined as *the application of experimentally derived laws of learning to human behavior*. Behavior modification is the result of years of scientific research conducted in laboratories and in natural settings, not just someone's hunch or unproven theory. What this boils down to is that everything that has been demonstrated about human learning is, by definition, a part of behavior modification. When we think about it, behavior modification is always going on. We are always learning, unlearning, and relearning various behaviors, but most learning is random and inefficient. Many people think behavior modification sounds very complicated and that they could never learn its principles or be able to apply these principles systematically. But once they start to become familiar with basic principles of behavior modification they begin to realize that it often seems like common sense applied in a systematic and efficient manner.

Applied behavior analysis is one of several subcategories of behavior modification, along with behavior therapy, programmed instruction, precision teaching, and others. Many of the classroom behavior management techniques that have been commonly used in classrooms for several decades now, such as contingency contracting and point systems, when done right, are applications of ABA methods and procedures. But behavior modification does not include drugs, psychosurgery, unproven theories or wishful thinking.

Target behaviors   While people are performing or *emitting* (as we sometimes say) behavior all the time, there are usually only a few behaviors that we are particularly interested in paying close attention to. Those behaviors targeted for change are often called *target behaviors*. A target behavior isn't necessarily a behavior we want to get rid of. It could also be an appropriate behavior that we want to strengthen.

Response   Sometimes we see or hear the word *response*. In general usage response is pretty much the same thing as behavior. But response in ABA usually refers to a behavior that immediately and predictably follows something in the environment.

Trial   A *trial* is the term for one try, attempt, repetition, or instance of a behavior, often in a situation set up to teach the behavior. Trial also sometimes refers to a set of more than one instance of the behavior. Usually many trials are needed to really learn something well. (Practice! Practice! Practice!)

Maladaptive behavior   Behaviorists often describe behavior as being adaptive or maladaptive. Adaptive behaviors are usually useful socially acceptable behaviors that are effective or functional in serving their purpose. They usually work and they usually don't hurt anybody. On the other hand *maladaptive behaviors* are behaviors that are not effective in achieving their goal and/or have other unwanted consequences. They may be socially or otherwise unacceptable because of their short- or long-term consequences for the individual who performs these behaviors or for their consequences or effects on others.

Verbal behavior   A very important ability that most humans have is the ability to use language to communicate with each other. Unfortunately, when this ability is hindered in some way it can make life very difficult. Communication ability is often seriously impaired in individuals with ASDs, but also for others with various forms of speech problems and certain learning disabilities. Behaviorists use the term *verbal behavior* (from Skinner's 1957 book of the same name, *Verbal Behavior*, which is considered one of his most important books) to refer not just to spoken language, but to other forms of communication as well, such as reading and writing. Sign language is a type of verbal behavior. Verbal behavior is such an important area, that *ABA International* has a journal entitled *The Analysis of Verbal Behavior* devoted exclusively to this topic.

As long as we're talking about verbal behavior, here are a few more terms that might come in handy to know.

Mand   A *mand* is a request. When using verbal behavior terminology in talking about verbal behavior, mand pretty much means to ask for something. Think of de-mand and com-mand, but not necessarily so emphatically. Mands are particularly easy to teach since they directly benefit the speaker by helping speakers to more easily get what they want. If Dick wants Jane to pass him the remote control, he might just say "Give me the remote control," which would be a mand.

Tact   *Tact* is another verbal behavior term that essentially means to name or label something. If Jane refers to a furry little animal with a long tail that says "meow" as a "kittie," she has tacted the cat. If Jane is looking through a picture book and sees a picture of a cookie, points to the cookie and says "Cookie," Jane has tacted the cookie. On the other hand when Jane is looking for a snack she might go up to her mother and say "Cookie!" Now that's a mand. Are you still with me? Remember, given the situation and function it serves, the same bit of verbal behavior could be a mand or could be a tact, sort of like the same word could be a verb or a noun, like *step* or *phone*, depending how you use it.

Covert behavior   In everyday chit chat when we're talking about behavior, we usually think of behavior that can be noticed or observed by just about anyone paying attention. Behavior of this sort is sometimes described as being public or overt behavior, since it is at least potentially directly observable by the public. In the behavioral world the term *covert behavior* refers to behavior such as thinking, imaging and feeling that is not directly observable to the public. Other actions inside our bodies, such as heart beats or brain waves, are also considered covert behavior. Since these private events can be observed directly by the individual experiencing them or indirectly through the use of medical instruments, they are considered behaviors as well.

Chapter 3

WHAT ARE ANTECEDENTS?

Stimulus   One of the terms that you'll probably hear quite a bit when you are listening to a behaviorist talk is the word *stimulus*. In general, a stimulus is something that stimulates or gets a reaction from something else. A stimulus is often something that can be noticed or detected by our senses. An object, an odor, a sound, an event we see happening, or most anything can be a stimulus.

Stimuli (plural for stimulus) that don't seem to affect behavior at all are called neutral stimuli. But there are many different kinds of stimuli that do affect our behavior in different ways. Stimuli that strengthen a behavior are called reinforcing stimuli and we'll talk a lot more about them in Chapter 4.

Antecedents   By *antecedents* or antecedent stimuli we mean things that happen or are already in place before the target behavior occurs. As we just said, many things going on don't seem to have any effect at all on the target behavior and are essentially neutral, at least as far as the target behavior is concerned. Other antecedents may signal that a particular behavior is likely to be reinforced or punished. A classic example is when a dinner bell or the cook's call that dinner is ready signals that if you go to the dining room, your behavior of going to the dining room is likely to be *reinforced* or rewarded with a good meal. Go to the dining room some other time, no food, no reinforcement. The dinner bell stimulus helps us to discriminate or tell the difference between the times that we will get a meal if we go to the dining room and the times that we won't get a meal. So the dinner bell in this case functions, operates, or works as a signal or cue called a *discriminative stimulus*.

Discriminative stimulus   Sulzer and Mayer (1972) described a *discriminative stimulus* as "a stimulus in the presence of which a given response is reinforced" (p.290). In some books you may see the symbol S^D, or S^d, used to stand for discriminative stimulus (with the D or d often printed as a superscript), or you might hear a speaker talking about an "Ess Dee." The speaker is simply pronouncing the initial letters, S and D, which really are a lot easier to say. Other terms like cue, sign, and signal are less formal, but convey the same general idea as S^D.

The S^D in the case of the dinner bell helps us to discriminate or notice when a particular behavior is likely to be reinforced, but an S^D could also signal that a behavior is likely to be punished. (In the case of the dinner bell, suppose liver is being served and you hate liver. Some people would consider being given a plate of liver to be punishment.) A red traffic light is an S^D that signals that driving through an intersection at that time is likely to be punished, possibly by an accident or perhaps by getting a traffic ticket if the police are watching.

Antecedents that affect behavior can come in a variety of forms. An antecedent to a target behavior could be someone else's behavior, such as a teacher telling Jane to open her math book. It might be a sign in a school directing visitors to report to the office. Words in a book are S^Ds for the students' reading behavior. Often the same stimulus can occasion or help bring about different behaviors from different individuals. For example, a sign on a highway that says "Dennisport, Exit 9" will influence different drivers differently. Those drivers who want to go to Dennisport are much more likely to get off the highway at Exit 9, while those wanting to go on to Provincetown will just keep on driving along.

A math worksheet given to a student is an antecedent that influences student behavior too. The teacher wants the presence of the worksheet, perhaps together with verbal instructions, to influence the student to complete the math problems. If this does happen then the math paper and verbal instructions are S^Ds for the desired behavior, doing the math problems. This will typically be the result. But before new behaviors are well established the intended eventual S^D often isn't strong enough to consistently lead to the desired behavior. The student may engage in some other, perhaps disruptive, type of behavior such as complaining or tantruming. Sometimes, besides the S^D additional cues or *prompts* are needed to get the ball rolling. When Jane is acting in a school play and forgets a line, the director might whisper the first words to Jane to get her started, or when Dick forgets the state capitals, his teacher might give him the hint that the capital of Rhode Island begins with "P." We should really think of these prompts as extra artificial S^Ds that are temporary aids that over time can be faded or reduced and eventually eliminated. It's like giving an extra clue or hint in a guessing game.

There are also discriminative stimuli called S-delta ("Ess Delta," represented by the symbol S^Δ) that indicate that a particular behavior will *not* be reinforced. If there is a sign on the door of a shop that says "Open at 2" and you try to get in at 11:30, chances are that you will find the door locked and your attempt to open that door will not be reinforced by success. You are not punished for trying to open the door, but you are not reinforced either.

Jane is about to take a computerized one-minute math test. She will be shown a series of subtraction problems all involving numbers less than 100. As each new problem appears on the computer screen she must quickly type in her answer to the problem and the next problem immediately appears. Jane will earn one reward point for each correct answer. After one minute the color of the numbers on the screen change from green to red. Although Jane can continue to type in answers after the color changes from green to red, Jane does not receive any more reward points no matter how many correct answers she types in, as long as the numbers are red. In this case green numbers are an S^D that correct answers will be reinforced, and red numbers are an S^Δ (S-delta) that correct answers will not be reinforced.

Stimulus control   When a behavior is clearly influenced so that it consistently occurs when its S^D is there, but doesn't happen or at least doesn't happen the same way without the S^D, we sometimes say the behavior is under *stimulus control*. Dick's mom may have been working on his manners by trying to teach him to say "Please" and "Thank you." When Mom is with him he remembers and follows through. When she is not around he forgets to say "Thank you." Dick's polite "Thank you" behavior is still under the stimulus control of his mother.

Setting event   While many of the antecedents we have talked about so far have been behaviors performed by others, the term *setting event* refers to other kinds of antecedents, including our bodily states and the presence of inanimate objects, that influence behavior as well. For example, someone being very hungry or very tired as opposed to having just eaten a big meal or having had a good night's sleep are certainly bodily states that can affect behavior in different ways. When you're hungry at 5:00 that is a setting event that makes it more likely that you'll eat a big dinner when dinner is served at 5:30. Another term that is being more widely used to describe pretty much the same idea as setting event is establishing operation.

Establishing operation (EO)   When something happens to make something else more or less reinforcing it is sometimes called an *establishing operation* (EO). An EO can be a naturally occurring event or it can be something that is intentionally arranged. This can be doing something to increase the ability of the stimuli we hope to use as reinforcers to really work as reinforcers, or it could be doing things to weaken the reinforcing ability of the reinforcers maintaining the maladaptive behavior.

EOs can be confused with S^Ds. (Remember them?) It might help to remember that EOs have to do with how much we might be reinforced by something (sort of like motivation) while S^Ds have to do with whether or not that reinforcer is potentially available to us (opportunity).

EOs often involve establishing states of deprivation or satiation (having too little or too much of something). For example, keeping with the food/eating theme, rather than going grocery shopping just before dinner, weight-conscious adults might be wise to do their grocery shopping right after dinner, thereby strengthening their ability to resist any temptations to buy (and eat) extra snack food, desserts, and the like. By eating just before shopping we have temporarily weakened (or abolished, as some would say) food as an effective reinforcer. We may say that eating dinner before grocery shopping is our establishing operation to make goodies at the grocery store easier to avoid.

Following up an earlier example, if we intend to use food as a reinforcer during Dick's math class, we probably want to be sure that he hasn't eaten for a while before math class. If Dick is hungry he's more likely to work for food and we have established food as a more powerful reinforcer in this situation. So to help something become more effective as a reinforcer we want to be sure that Dick hasn't had too much of that reinforcer lately. We also want to be sure that, at least for the time being, the only way that Dick can get this particular reinforcer is by performing the new behavior that we want him to perform.

An EO that would be likely to make something less effective as a reinforcer would be to make the reinforcer noncontingently or freely available to Jane. In other words Jane still gets the reinforcer no matter what she does or doesn't do. For example, suppose Dick and Jane are outside playing. Dick is playing with his basketball and Jane is playing with a soccer ball. Dick asks Jane to play basketball with him, but Jane declines because she wants to continue to play soccer. As they continue to play by themselves, the temperature begins to drop and both are getting cold. Dick escapes from the cold by putting on both the sweater and jacket that he has with him, but Jane has neither and is still getting colder. So Dick tells Jane that if she will play basketball with him she can borrow his jacket. Reluctantly, Jane agrees. After they play basketball for a few minutes their mother comes along with a sweater in her hand and calls to Jane: "Jane, it's cold out, come and put your sweater on!" This can be thought of as an establishing operation in that by providing Jane with a sweater to keep warm, regardless of what she does, Mother has more or less neutralized the reinforcing ability of Dick's jacket in this situation. Now with a sweater of her own, Dick's jacket is no longer a powerful enough reinforcer to keep Jane playing basketball. Wearing her own sweater, Jane goes back to playing soccer. In this story the reinforcing value of Dick's jacket is first increased by the naturally occurring EO of the drop in temperature. Then, when Mother comes along with Jane's sweater, which is another EO in this situation, the reinforcing value of Dick's jacket drops again. This sounds like some stock I once owned. If you have a tendency to think of things from a criminal point of view, you might think of an establishing operation as setting up a mark.

In recent years some behavior analysts have introduced a newer term, *motivating operation* (MO), to describe the same general idea as EO. While there are some technical differences, for our purposes we can think of an EO and an MO as pretty much the same thing.

Elicit and **emit**   Two other words that we often hear when behaviorists are talking about someone performing a behavior are *elicit* and *emit*. We say that a stimulus *elicits* a response or behavior when the behavior really has to happen, like in an involuntary reflex. You know, when the doctor whacks you on the knee with that little rubber hammer and you automatically kick, or when a sudden bright light elicits an eye blink. On the other hand sometimes a behavior occurs and we don't see anything that made it absolutely positively have to happen. Maybe we have no clue as to why Dick did whatever he did, and it appears to be a more voluntary behavior, even if it is influenced by its consequences. In these situations someone might say Dick *emitted* the behavior. While sitting next to Jane in church on Sunday perhaps Dick reaches out his hand and starts tickling Jane. Did he really have to do that? No. Did he do it? Yes. Dick emitted the tickling behavior.

Chapter 4

WHAT ARE CONSEQUENCES?

Consequences   When we talk about *consequences*, we're talking about what happens next after the target behavior occurs, usually immediately after. Things that follow a behavior with a certain degree of regularity often begin to have an effect on how frequently the behavior that they follow occurs. The process through which these consequences influence behavior is called *operant conditioning*.

Operant conditioning   *Operant conditioning*, sometimes called operant learning, is the most common of the various ways in which learning takes place. In operant conditioning the frequency with which a certain behavior occurs depends on what happens right after it occurs, that is, the behavior's immediate *consequences*. Doesn't that sound kind of familiar? *Operant conditioning* is the underlying principle of most of the behavior modification techniques used in ABA. Although some examples will be included, our emphasis will be on basic principles and guidelines so that you can then adapt them to your own unique needs. If you happen to be a psychology major or graduate student in a field related to psychology or if you just really want to learn a lot about operant conditioning, I recommend a book entitled *Primer of Operant Conditioning* by G. S. Reynolds. According to Reynolds, "*operant conditioning* refers to a process in which the frequency of occurrence of a bit of behavior is modified by the consequences of the behavior" (Reynolds 1968, p.1). Basically it's the idea that behavior is a function of its consequences, or that whatever you do is strongly influenced by the events that follow the behavior, by what happens right after you do it.

   If something you like happens (for example, the peppermint candy you ate tasted really good to you), your behavior has probably been reinforced and you're a bit more likely to do the same thing again sometime (you will probably reach for another piece of peppermint candy). If something you don't like happens (for example, you don't like the licorice candy you ate), you are less likely to do the same thing again (you will probably not reach for a second licorice candy). When talking with behaviorists, it is important to remember that it is behavior, not people, that is reinforced.

Positive reinforcement When the consequences of behavior are such that they make the behavior more likely to occur again in the future, we call it *positive reinforcement*. Usually the reinforcer is something that the reinforced individual experiences as pleasurable or rewarding, like a hot fudge sundae. The reinforcer can come in either tangible or intangible form, such as a piece of candy or a smile from someone we like. It can be very tempting to call a reinforcer a reward. Rewards are often reinforcing, but not always. But we can't assume in advance that a reward intended to be a reinforcer will actually work as a reinforcer. Believe it or not, there are a few people here and there who actually don't like hot fudge sundaes!

If you are familiar with the literature in this area, you might find the term *Law of Effect* (developed by E. L. Thorndike in the early 1900s) used to emphasize the importance of the actual effects of behavior in the learning process. An example of the learning operation of positive reinforcement could involve Dick calling out in class without raising his hand. If Dick gets what he wants, the attention of the teacher and/or his classmates, then he has been reinforced for calling out and will be more likely to call out again in the future. Reinforcing a behavior that we want to happen again is the best way to increase its strength and frequency. If Dick were in a situation where nobody paid any attention to him when he called out, but he could get attention by raising his hand first, he would soon stop calling out and begin raising his hand.

Sometimes people talk about learning by trial and error. Trial and success is a better name for this process. We try behaving in different ways until we find something that works to get the consequence or result we want. The behavior that is finally successful in getting the desired help is positively reinforced. The underlying idea of positive reinforcement is to "catch them being good," and reinforce Jane's good behavior.

Depending on how you look at it, there can be lots of different kinds of reinforcers, and sometimes the terminology used in describing them can be confusing. And, I hate to say it, but not all of the "experts" use these terms exactly the same way, so that can make it even more confusing. Here are some of the terms that are used to differentiate different types of reinforcers and what these terms commonly mean. I already mentioned that reinforcers can be tangible or intangible. Sometimes we hear talk about *primary* and *secondary* or *conditioned* reinforcers.

Primary reinforcer   A *primary reinforcer* is reinforcing for itself. Primary reinforcers are generally things that help keep us alive. Food or water is naturally reinforcing to just about everyone who is hungry or thirsty. (The states of being hungry and thirsty are setting events.)

Secondary reinforcer, conditioned reinforcer   *Secondary* or *conditioned reinforcers* such as verbal praise or compliments (or merit badges or awards) are not intrinsically reinforcing themselves, but only begin to work as reinforcers after they become associated with primary reinforcers that often follow them. Sometimes people themselves become conditioned reinforcers, as the sources through which other reinforcers are received. Grandparents who love to shower their grandchildren with lots of gifts are examples of individuals who commonly become powerful conditioned reinforcers.

   Another distinction sometimes made is between extrinsic and intrinsic reinforcers.

Extrinsic reinforcers   *Extrinsic reinforcers* are generally tangible or otherwise observable consequences. These are the reinforcers that we can usually see, feel, touch and so forth.

Intrinsic reinforcers   Sometimes, however, the act of doing something may be reinforcing by itself and we say that it is intrinsically reinforcing or an *intrinsic reinforcer*. Creative activities are often considered to be intrinsically reinforcing. For Dick, playing his guitar is intrinsically reinforcing. For Jane, maybe painting a picture of some flowers is intrinsically reinforcing. You don't have to add any artificial consequences to get Dick to practice his guitar, or Jane to paint; you just give them the opportunity.

Automatic reinforcement   Reinforcement that doesn't include any social interaction with others is sometimes called *automatic reinforcement*. Cigarette smoking reinforced by the effects of nicotine and self-stimulating behavioral patterns are examples of automatic reinforcement and many self-injurious behaviors (SIBs) are maintained by automatic reinforcement. Other behavior patterns, such as the prolonged rocking and hand flapping that are sometimes seen in children with various forms of autism, are likely to be examples of automatic reinforcement as well. Since many children with ASDs do not seem to be as sensitive to social reinforcers as others, automatic reinforcement becomes more powerful for them.

   Even though some of these behaviors (such as self-biting and eye poking) can eventually result in considerable harm to the child engaging in them, these long-term consequences are outweighed by their immediate short-term consequences such as anxiety reduction or other physiological responses that seem to keep these maladaptive behaviors going strong. For just all of us, scratching an itch can be thought of as automatic reinforcement.

Social reinforcement   *Social reinforcement* is a type of secondary reinforcement that involves getting attention from others. Depending on the social circumstances and who the attention is coming from, their attention may or may not be reinforcing. The same event can involve both primary and secondary reinforcement. When I was in graduate school one of my professors, Joe Cautela, loved to go out to eat with groups of his colleagues and students. We often found ourselves at a seafood restaurant and Joe always seemed to have a bucket of clams in front of him. As the conversation around the table went on, Joe would pass out clams as reinforcers when someone made a comment that he particularly liked. So the clams were primary reinforcers if you were hungry and liked clams, but they were also secondary reinforcers because of what they represented, acknowledgement that the master thought you said something smart, and that you were receiving his attention and approval.

Generalized reinforcer   Another type of reinforcer is a *generalized reinforcer*, such as money. In addition to being a conditioned reinforcer, generalized reinforcers such as money, tokens, stars, chips, points and the like can have the reinforcing effect of the various reinforcers for which they can be exchanged.

Backup reinforcer   Generalized reinforcers would not be effective for long unless they had *backup reinforcers* that can be received in exchange for the generalized reinforcers. These backup reinforcers (e.g. a TV, car, clothes, toys, books, snacks, privileges, etc.) are what the generalized reinforcers can buy.

Edibles   When a bit of food is used as a reinforcer it is often referred to as an edible. Usually small pieces of food, such as M&Ms, nuts, crackers, grapes and the like, are used as edibles. In the grand scheme of things, using food, particularly candy and the less healthy stuff, is intended as a temporary situation that can, it is hoped, eventually be replaced by social reinforcers or natural reinforcers.

Contrived reinforcement   *Contrived reinforcement* is a term used by Skinner to refer to specially arranged artificial consequences to behavior. Reinforcers that do not follow *naturally* from the behavior are contrived, whether we are talking about giving Dick an M&M for staying in his chair for five minutes, letting Jane watch 30 minutes of TV after completing her homework, or giving you a paycheck on Friday afternoon after you've gone to work all week.

In many cases the hope is that contrived reinforcement will be a temporary thing until natural reinforcers take over and maintain the behavior. This is when something involved in the act itself may be intrinsically reinforcing, such as when an artist or other crafts person is reinforced by the act of painting or working at their craft and by the enjoyment of their finished product. In teaching social behavior we may need to use contrived reinforcers to get Jane to start conversations or play with classmates, regardless of how awkward her first attempts are. As time goes by and she becomes more socially skilled, it is hoped that the natural consequences of the reactions of her peers will continue to maintain her increasingly skilled behavior and the contrived reinforcers can be phased out (like with those edibles we just talked about).

As long as we are talking about reinforcement and reinforcers, there are a few more important points we need to keep in mind. First, reinforcers are idiosyncratic. That is, they are highly individualized and personal. What works as a reinforcer for you may not work as a reinforcer for me. Different strokes for different folks. We all have different tastes. Dick might prefer anchovies on his pizza while mushrooms work better for Jane. Personally, I never met a pizza I didn't like.

Satiation A second important consideration has to do with our state of *satiation* or deprivation with regard to the intended reinforcer. Most of the time chocolate ice cream may be a positive reinforcer for most people. But if you've just had a three-scoop chocolate ice cream cone and a big piece of chocolate cake at a birthday party, you may have had more than your fill of chocolate for now. You are satiated. If you had to eat more chocolate then, instead of being a reinforcer, it might be more of a punisher. But after time passes you eventually recover your taste for chocolate and it functions, or works, as a reinforcer again. As time continues to pass and you still do not get your chocolate, you may feel deprived of chocolate, even crave chocolate, and in this state of deprivation, chocolate could be a very powerful reinforcer.

So sometimes in some situations a particular stimulus is a reinforcer and at other times or in other situations the same thing can be useless or, worse still, have an unpleasant, aversive effect. It may actually punish or reduce the behavior we were hoping to strengthen. This can be pretty confusing. In everyday life we are dealing with generalized reinforcers like money so it's easy to see how we can get in the habit of thinking of something that is sometimes a reinforcer as always being a reinforcer. (After all, isn't money almost always reinforcing for almost everyone?) But the truth is that rather than defining a reinforcer as the object or situation itself, we have to consider what effect it has, how it functions or works in a particular situation, to determine whether or not it truly is a reinforcer, here and now. We can not take it for granted that once a reinforcer, always a reinforcer. There's an old saying in ABA that "A reinforcer is only a reinforcer if it reinforces." When we get to Chapter 6 we'll talk about ways to figure out what might make a good reinforcer and what might not. The bottom line is: if the consequence of the behavior makes it more likely that the behavior will occur again, the behavior has been reinforced. Even if we gave someone a million dollars to perform the behavior, if the behavior isn't more likely to occur again, then it was not reinforced.

So satiation is another term you are likely to hear from time to time because it is really an important concept. Remember, if we want our intended reinforcers to be effective we need to be alert to when Dick or Jane starts to tire of them and get bored, so we can make helpful changes. The good news is that after a while without those tired old former reinforcers, they sometimes recover their reinforcing abilities. Absence makes the heart grow fonder.

Habituation *Habituation* is basically getting used to something. Usually new or novel stimuli get our attention more than they do after they have been around for a while and become the "same old same old." Sometimes habituation is for the better, like when we get desensitized to a previously aversive stimulus, such as getting used to a bad smell or an annoying background noise. On the other hand we also get used to and are sometimes indifferent about things that we like and which once may have been usable as positive reinforcers. Remember satiation?

Some behaviorists like to think of reinforcers that motivate people to act in various ways as falling into four categories: These are reinforcers that are tangible objects, reinforcers that involve sensory stimulation, reinforcers that include social attention from others, and a type of reinforcement that involves escape or avoidance from unpleasant circumstances called negative reinforcement, and that's what we will talk about next.

Negative reinforcement In addition to positive reinforcement, there is another kind of reinforcement called *negative reinforcement*. A very common misunderstanding is to confuse negative reinforcement with punishment. They are not the same thing. Actually, negative reinforcement is quite different from punishment, which we will talk more about in a few pages. *Negative reinforcement does not weaken behavior.* Negative reinforcement is rather a second operation through which the frequency of a behavior is actually increased or strengthened. In negative reinforcement, behavior is increased by stopping an unpleasant or *aversive* condition as soon as the desired behavior occurs. Instead of presenting or adding something pleasant, we remove or subtract something unpleasant. A classic example of negative reinforcement involves seatbelt safety systems built into many cars in years past. If you started the engine before having your seatbelt buckled, an annoying alarm buzzer would go off and in many cases continue buzzing until you either fastened your seatbelt or turned off the engine. By buckling their seatbelts, drivers and passengers were able to put an end to the annoying aversive sound and ride along in peace and quiet. Motorists were then more likely to fasten their seatbelts in the future and their seatbelt-fastening behavior had been negatively reinforced.

There are also many examples of negative reinforcement involving social interactions. Who has not seen (or experienced first hand) a child in a supermarket who keeps pestering a parent to buy this or that until the embarrassed parent is worn down and eventually gives in? Another example is the mother who learns that she can stop her baby's crying, which most people would consider an aversive situation, by going to the baby whenever she begins to cry. Since Mother is being negatively reinforced by the end of the crying, chances are she will end up going to the baby more and more when the baby cries. But there are two sides to everything. Mother may be learning that by going to Baby Jane when Jane is crying she can stop Jane's crying right away. Baby Jane, on the other hand, is also learning that she can get positive reinforcement, her mother's attention, anytime she wants to simply by crying, and in the long run she will probably cry even more often than before.

In schools it is common to see students who have learned to keep pestering, trying this approach with their teacher, often with mixed results. In the real world (or *natural environment*, as behaviorists like to call it) negative reinforcement is often a two-way street. The person who is negatively reinforced for doing whatever they did to end the unpleasant situation has just reinforced the unwanted behavior of the other person who was making the situation unpleasant in the first place.

Dick might really hate reading aloud in class. When his teacher says to the class "Take out your reading book now, we are going to read aloud the story starting on page twenty-five," Dick starts disrupting the class by pushing the papers off the desk of the student sitting next to him. The teacher sees this and sends Dick out of the class. This removes what to the teacher is an aversive stimulus, Dick's behavior. But it also enables Dick to get away from what to him is aversive, that is, having to read aloud in class. Consequently, Dick will probably be more likely to act up again the next time oral reading comes along. So both Dick and his teacher have been negatively reinforced, Dick by acting up and getting out of oral reading, and the teacher by throwing Dick out of class and not having to put up with his disruptive behavior (at least not for now).

It can be really helpful to think through these situations from the other person's point of view. A friend told me a story about his grandmother and their family dog. The dog used to spend a lot of time begging at the dinner table. This annoyed Grandma to no end. Thinking that she would get the dog to go away, Grandma would often give old "Lucky Dog" a bit of food, usually a piece of meat, from the table. Lucky immediately took the food away and enjoyed her snack in private while briefly giving Grandma a break. But Lucky would soon be back, looking for more. After enjoying her few moments of relief from Lucky's begging, Grandma would become frustrated again, saying something like "I don't understand why that dog's here again, I gave her what she wanted!" In this case we had two good examples of reinforcement. First, Grandma's unintentional use of positive reinforcement to reinforce Lucky's begging at the table, which, as you probably guessed, increased. Second, Lucky, by immediately (but briefly) leaving the table area, used negative reinforcement to get Grandma to give her more snacks from the table.

Escape   There are two types of negative reinforcement. The first is *escape,* in which the behavior puts an end to an already existing aversive situation. When the alarm buzzer goes off on a clock in the morning we reach over and turn it off to escape from the annoying noise. (If we really want to make the alarm clock more effective, the alarm should be placed out of reach of the bed to get more *waking behavior* from us and make it even less likely that we'll fall back to sleep after we turn it off.) If a sudden rain storm comes up while children are playing outside, they quickly run for cover to escape from the cold, wet rain.

Avoidance   The second type of negative reinforcement is called *avoidance.* In this case we behave in a certain way to avoid the aversive event before it occurs. Dick might turn around and walk in another direction when he sees a bully ahead. The use of caller ID features on telephones is negatively reinforced by avoiding unwanted calls. If we are driving along a bit too fast and spot a police car on the side of the road ahead, chances are we'll slow down to avoid getting a ticket. Much of the legal system is based on avoidance. We do or do not do certain things to avoid legal consequences such as fines, jail and other aversive consequences.

With older children and adolescents we can often see negative reinforcement at work in peer pressure situations. A high school student might be teased by his or her peers until finally giving in, to escape from the teasing, and begin smoking or drinking. Others may join in to avoid the teasing altogether.

To help understand the difference between escape and avoidance, think of what might happen if you are outside when it starts raining. You begin to get wet, and to *escape* from getting wet, you put up your umbrella, if you're lucky enough to have one with you, or perhaps you find shelter under an overhang, or maybe you go back indoors. You were getting wet, for a while, which may have been aversive to you, but then you escaped from the aversive situation. Perhaps after you've been caught in the rain a few times you've learned that when you see rain clouds in the sky it's a good idea to take an umbrella with you when you go out if you want to *avoid* getting wet. If it actually does begin to rain you can now *avoid* getting wet at all by getting that umbrella up before it rains enough to get you wet. These are both examples of negative reinforcement, escape and avoidance.

Besides these operations that increase behavior there are three operations that decrease behavior.

Extinction   If we want to decrease the frequency of a particular behavior we should make sure that when the target behavior does occur, nothing follows it that would encourage or reinforce it. The process through which behavior is eliminated by withholding reinforcement is called *extinction*. If nobody laughs (positive reinforcer) when we tell jokes, chances are our joke-telling behavior will soon become a thing of the past (extinguished). It is common to see teachers ignoring students who call out answers in class without raising their hands. This is what the mother mentioned earlier might have done when little Jane began whining (assuming, of course, that Mother was satisfied there wasn't any appropriate reason for Jane's whining).

Extinction burst   In an ideal situation extinction is a good way to deal with tantrums. But it often takes a great deal of patience to extinguish behavior. Sometimes a person who is on an extinction schedule (i.e. he is no longer receiving reinforcement for a particular behavior) shows a temporary increase in the frequency and intensity of the target behavior before the behavior decreases. Dick may have learned that he can get his mother's attention by whining. But one day whining no longer works, so he whines even more strongly at first before he tires and gives up. This temporary increase is called an *extinction burst*. Unfortunately, this is where many people make their mistake. Dick's parents think the extinction isn't working and they give up when the target behavior (whining) increases (before it begins to decrease) and they give Dick whatever he wants to quiet him down. While Dick usually quiets down in the short run, his parents are actually reinforcing and strengthening the very behavior they are trying to get rid of! Dick has in effect learned that his old amount of whining is no longer effective and that if he wants to be reinforced he must resort to even longer and perhaps more intense episodes of whining for it to pay off. He has learned to perform at a higher level for the same or even less reinforcement. This is quite unfortunate since, with just a little more patience by his parents, Dick would have learned that whining was no longer an effective means of getting his own way. Now that his whining behavior has been cycled upward, it will take even longer to extinguish the whining if his parents try extinction again.

Extinction takes time and should not be attempted if you cannot allow enough time to extinguish the target behavior. You must be patient. If you try extinction and fail, chances are that the target behavior will only get worse. Actually, you are better off not attempting extinction if you can not put up with a temporary increase in the behavior, if you are not sure you can outwait the behavior, if the behavior is hurting someone, or if you are not sure you can be consistent.

Extinction is one of the most commonly attempted and goofed up procedures. When used properly, extinction should be used in combination with positive reinforcement of the appropriate behavior that you want to replace the troublesome behavior. Eliminating one way of receiving reinforcement without providing an acceptable alternative way to maintain the child's general level of reinforcement is looking for trouble. The child will seek reinforcement in other ways, and if we don't provide an acceptable way, chances are the child will develop another bad habit. Nonbehaviorists might call this *symptom substitution*.

If it is practical to use extinction in a given situation, using it in combination with reinforcement of an incompatible response is usually the best way to eliminate an unwanted behavior. For example, if we want to stop Jane from calling out in class, we should not only remove any reinforcement she gets for calling out (attention), but we should reinforce her for periods of quiet behavior, such as doing her work sheets. Since she can't be both calling out and quiet at the same time, and it is now being quiet that pays off, Jane will be much more likely to keep quiet.

In operant learning there are two additional means of decreasing undesirable behavior.

Punishment In *punishment* the unwanted behavior is immediately followed by the presentation of an aversive consequence which results in a decrease in the frequency of the behavior that immediately preceded it. A classic but not recommended example could be spanking Dick for talking back to his parents. In a school setting, punishment might take the form of speaking sternly to Dick or having him write "I will not hit my classmates" 50 times. Although punishment sometimes appears to work, research has shown that the results of punishment are inconsistent and quite often include unwanted side effects, including the possibility of accidentally strengthening the target behavior.

One of the most controversial areas in behavior modification is the use of aversive control, particularly punishment. Many people are opposed to the use of punishment on ethical grounds. For others this is not a problem. And still others avoid the use of punishment as much as possible because of the practical problem of the many undesirable side effects it can have. Murray Sidman wrote a terrific book called *Coercion and its Fallout* (1989), which discusses the use of punishment and the problems it can lead to in great detail.

Whether you are ethically for or against punishment, since punishment is used widely in educational settings, it might be worthwhile to mention some of the problems we can get into by using punishment.

First, one of the problems with using punishment is that experience and research both have found that punishment tends to suppress rather than eliminate behavior. What this means is that the punished individual may learn to not perform the punished behavior as long as the threat of punishment seems real, but once the likelihood of being punished goes away the punished behavior often comes back. It might have been temporarily suppressed or held down, but not eliminated. Using punishment is a good way to accidentally teach people to be sneaky.

Second, the effects of punishment often seem to be specific to the situations in which it is applied. There is less generalization to other situations than there usually is when positive reinforcement is used. Perhaps you know of a driver who tends to drive a bit over the speed limit. But our friend may have received a speeding ticket from the police along a particular stretch of highway. Now, although he often slows down to the posted speed limit when he drives through that section of road, he still typically drives a bit over the speed limit just about everywhere else. Sort of like kids doing *naughty* things when they can get away with it, such as swearing when no adult is around.

Behavioral contrast   Actually, if a behavior is punished and suppressed in one situation, it may even increase in other situations where it is not punished. This is called *behavioral contrast*. Behavior that is suppressed in one setting may increase over its normal level in other settings. For example, suppose Dick throws an average of ten spitballs per class. In one class the teacher might use punishment to hold him down to three or four spitballs. When Dick gets in the next class, though, he might be up to 16 or 17 spitballs.

Third, the location in which the punishment occurs can also become aversive to the person who was punished there. How often do we hear stories about people who don't want to return to places where bad things happened to them? Their unpleasant emotional responses to these locations can make them go to great lengths to avoid returning to "the scene of the crime," so to speak. Even when the geographical location of the aversive event really had nothing to do with it, it can still become a place to be avoided. Jane's avoidance of the girls' bathroom at school may have its roots in her having been teased by an older girl in the bathroom last year. Although the older girl has now moved on to another school, Jane is still very uneasy in the same school bathroom.

Fourth, the adult doing the punishing often becomes aversive to the child being punished, which makes it difficult for this adult to control that child's behavior in any other way. Remember earlier we talked about grandparents becoming conditioned reinforcers? In the same way the bestowers of punishment can become aversive stimuli themselves, bringing about fear and dislike from those that they punish. Often a school disciplinarian, such as a particularly strict assistant principal, falls into this trap. Once this happens, it becomes much more difficult for that individual to be effective using positive controls with students.

Fifth, some types of punishment are similar to behaviors we actually want to increase, or encourage a liking for. Assigning an extra page of math problems as a punishment risks unintentionally strengthening what might already be an aversion to math, certainly an unwanted side effect. If math is presented as a punishment, doing math may become even more unpleasant and result in much less math being done in the long run.

Sixth, some attempts at punishment may not be aversive to the person we are trying to punish. If Dick is told to stay after school with a teacher he likes for throwing something in class, he may be more likely to throw more stuff in class. Just as not every intended reinforcer is reinforcing to everyone, the same can be said for intended punishments. I remember a popular English teacher in my high school days way back in the last century who was also one of the school's football coaches. It turned out that Mr. Fudd (not his real name, which has been changed to protect the innocent) was assigned as the after-school detention monitor on Mondays. During the fall football season, detention period on Mondays usually ended up being a 45-minute review of the highlights of that weekend's football game. Needless to say, the number of boys receiving detention on Mondays was much higher than the rest of the week as many students intentionally engaged in minor infractions of school rules to earn the intended punishment (but functional reinforcer) of detention on Monday afternoons.

Seventh, just as reinforcers tend to satiate and become less effective if overused, many punishments lose their effectiveness if used too much. Remember habituation? Some just seem to be outgrown. Whereas a reprimand might be effective with a primary grade student, by the time the student reaches the sixth or seventh grade, reprimanding just doesn't work so well any more.

Eighth, since using punishment often works quickly in the short run to suppress unwanted behavior (even if it actually increases the target behavior in the long run) the person doing the punishing usually is reinforced (remember negative reinforcement?) for using punishment and may be a bit more likely to quickly turn to punishment again in the future. Without realizing it, the adult can slip into a trap of delivering more and more punishment without really reducing the long-term frequency of the unwanted behavior.

These are just some of the problems that can arise using punishment. However, keeping these potential problems in mind, we should add that punishment can be useful to get behaviors that are dangerous, either to the child or someone else, quickly suppressed and under temporary control until slower-acting positive reinforcement can more effectively replace the dangerous behavior with more acceptable alternatives.

Response cost   Another procedure used to reduce behaviors is called *response cost*. Some people consider response cost to be a form of punishment, but without as many potential pitfalls. In response cost the undesirable behavior is followed by the loss or subtraction of something that the individual values. While this involves the immediate removal of something usually reinforcing, it is not the reinforcer for this particular target behavior. Paying a fine or a loss of privileges is a response cost. For example, a child who hits a classmate might lose his or her recess privilege for the day. Logically, response cost might be thought of as negative punishment (subtracting something nice and target behavior decreases). Response cost seems to be more effective and to have fewer undesirable side effects than punishment.

Trying to remember these five basic learning operations can be pretty tough sometimes. They can be confusing. Visualizing these operations on a grid, like Table 4.1, can make it easier to keep them straight.

Reinforcement schedules   Obviously, people usually cannot be reinforced every single time they do what we want them to do. At least their behaviors can't always be reinforced in the natural environment. It just isn't practical in most real-world situations. This brings us to the problem of scheduling reinforcement or *reinforcement schedules*.

Continuous reinforcement   When people receive reinforcement every time they perform a particular behavior, we say they are on a *continuous reinforcement* schedule. This is usually the quickest way to establish a new behavior. But continuous reinforcement is not necessary to maintain or keep behaviors going, and actually can be inefficient and not very practical. Once Dick is performing the desired behavior, the next step is to make sure that the new behavior is maintained, or becomes a regular habit. This is done through the use of any of a number of *intermittent* or *partial reinforcement* schedules.

Table 4.1 Learning operations

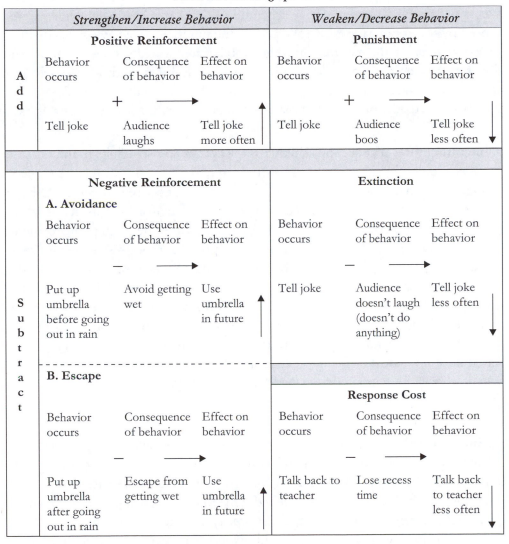

Intermittent reinforcement, partial reinforcement In *intermittent reinforcement* (or *partial reinforcement*, as it is sometimes called) the behavior is reinforced sometimes, but not always. There are four basic intermittent reinforcement schedules. Two of these schedules are based on the number of behaviors performed and the other two schedules are based on the length of time that has passed since the last reinforced behavior occurred.

Fixed ratio (FR) The first is the *fixed ratio* schedule in which the individual is always reinforced for the same number of times the target behavior happens. For example, a sales person might receive a bonus commission for every fourth pair of shoes sold. In class, a child may receive one star for each ten correct answers. Workers paid on a piecework pay schedule are on a fixed ratio schedule, represented by the abbreviation FR followed by the number of behaviors needed for reinforcement. If the requirement is assembling five widgets, then the abbreviation for this reinforcement or payment schedule is FR 5. Although fixed ratio schedules can be the simplest to use, we have to be careful that we don't sacrifice quality or accuracy for quantity or speed and end up with a lot of sloppy work.

Variable ratio (VR)   The second schedule is the *variable ratio* schedule. In the variable ratio schedule the number of responses required for reinforcement keeps changing, so that little Jane never knows when to expect reinforcement. She is always kept guessing. She might receive two or three reinforcements in a row and then have to give seven or eight responses before she gets her next reinforcement. Over time though there is an average of the number of responses needed for reinforcement. Once again, this can be represented by an abbreviation with the average number of behaviors used for reinforcement, such as VR 10. It is also the most powerful and effective of the basic reinforcement schedules. By that we mean fewer total reinforcements are necessary to keep the behaviors going and, as far as the basic schedules are concerned, behaviors maintained on a variable ratio schedule are the most difficult to extinguish. Not surprisingly, variable ratio is the schedule that the famous one-armed bandit slot machines in casinos appear to work on.

Fixed interval (FI)   The two schedules based on time are called *interval schedules*. In an interval schedule it does not matter how many times a behavior occurs, as long as it occurs at least once. What does matter is how much time has passed. If it takes ten minutes for a pot of water to boil, it doesn't matter how many times you check *before* that ten minutes are up. It's the first time *after* the ten minutes are up that you will be reinforced with boiling water. This would be a *fixed interval* schedule (FI 10, for ten minutes).

Variable interval (VI)   There are also *variable interval* schedules. Have you ever tried to reach someone by phone but kept getting a busy signal? We keep picking up and dialing with no way of knowing when the line will be free. It doesn't matter how many times we try. But that first successful attempt once the phone line is free gets reinforced. Since we don't know when we are going to get an answer and our attempts to complete calls may be successful sooner or later, our phone-calling behavior is reinforced on a variable interval (VI) schedule.

Sometimes we want to reinforce a continuous, ongoing behavior rather than individual responses. An example of continuous behavior could be reading in class. We don't want a lot of going off and on task; we want Dick to stick to it. In this case it would be better for us to use a *variable interval* reinforcement schedule. On a variable interval schedule, as with the variable ratio schedule, he never knows when the reinforcement is coming, only that he must be performing the behavior desired in order to be reinforced.

Thinning   The process by which we change schedules from continuous to partial is sometimes called *thinning*. Gradually, almost so that it isn't even noticed, the amount of desirable behavior required for reinforcement is increased, but at a rate slow enough so that the desirable behavior isn't extinguished due to lack of sufficient reinforcement.

The four basic intermittent reinforcement schedules are summarized below.

A. Based on the number of responses (behaviors)

1. Fixed ratio (FR)

- Reinforcement is delivered for every X number of responses, with X remaining constant.

- The person usually knows when the reinforcer will be delivered.

- For example, piecework.

- For example, a token contingent upon placing five pegs correctly in a board (FR 5).

2. Variable ratio (VR)

- Reinforcement delivered for every X number of responses with X varying.

- The person is kept guessing as to when the reinforcer will be delivered.

- Most efficient schedule (can usually get the most work for the smallest payoff).

- Toughest schedule with which to use extinction successfully.

- For example, one-armed bandit slot machine that is set to deliver one payoff on the average of ten attempts (VR 10).

B. *Based on the time elapsed since the last reinforced response*

   1. Fixed interval (FI)

   • Reinforcement delivered for first response after X time has elapsed, where X remains constant.

   • The number of responses during X has absolutely no effect on the delivery of reinforcement.

   • For example, checking to see the coffee is ready. (It doesn't matter how many times you check, the coffee won't be ready any sooner.)

   • If you boil a three-minute egg, it will always take three minutes (FI 3).

   2. Variable interval (VI)

   • Reinforcement delivered for first response after X time has elapsed, where X varies.

   • For example, trying to reach someone by telephone and the line is busy. (It doesn't matter how often you try and you can't know how soon the line will be free.)

   • Even if you go fishing every Thursday you don't know ahead of time how long it will take to catch your first fish. If you keep a record of this all summer long, however, you might find the average time is 15 minutes (VI 15).

Chapter 5

WHAT ARE SOME OTHER KINDS OF LEARNING?

Modeling So far we have been talking about direct learning. But in addition to the operant learning that we've already talked about, there is another kind of learning that has an especially strong influence on children. This kind of learning is called *modeling*. Sometimes referred to as *imitative, vicarious, observational* or *social learning*, modeling is the process through which an individual's behavior changes after observing someone else (called a model) perform the behavior, rather than by personally performing the behaviors and directly experiencing the consequences. Usually, the more the child admires the model or the more similar to the child the model appears, the more likely it is that the model's behavior will be imitated. For example, a number of children might start making noises in class after one child begins. Monkey see, monkey do. Or if an admired member of the class volunteers to help with a job, it will be easier to get others to do the same.

A teacher's demonstration of how to do something is a form of modeling. Modeling isn't limited to watching something happen and then copying what we just saw. Besides seeing people behave in real life and imitating them, watching real and fictional models on TV and in the movies, listening to CDs, radios, iPods, hearing a story with a moral to it, reading about characters in books, and other types of media are all ways that modeling can take place.

A considerable amount of research has been conducted and many books have been written about modeling by Albert Bandura and his associates (e.g. Bandura 1974). Although experts still disagree about just how learning takes place through modeling, for our practical purposes here modeling does work as a means to influence behavior, whether for better or worse. (If it didn't, why would so much money be put into TV commercials with actors modeling using and purchasing various products and celebrities telling us to buy this and buy that?)

Behavioral repertoire   A *behavioral repertoire* includes the behaviors that someone has the ability to currently perform, right now, but most of which are not being presently performed. Reading sentences in English is part of your behavioral repertoire and that is what you are doing right now. Swimming may also be in your behavioral repertoire, but unless you're really talented, you're not swimming right now. Flying the space shuttle probably is not in your behavioral repertoire, and it is definitely not in my behavioral repertoire either.

It is important to make the distinction between the acquisition of behavior and the performance of behavior. Acquisition has to do with learning how to perform a behavior that you could not previously do. You may not be able to play a tuba. If you wanted to play a tuba you would have to go through a long learning process of acquiring quite a few tuba-playing behaviors. But just because the ability to play a tuba is then in your behavioral repertoire, it obviously doesn't mean that you're constantly playing the tuba. The right conditions have to be in place to *motivate* you to perform the behavior. We all have many behavioral patterns in our repertoires that we could perform if the conditions were right, but we don't perform them all the time. You may be able to drive a car, but it is hoped you're not doing that now at the same time you are trying to read this. Once a behavior is acquired, we need to establish a system to encourage or *occasion* and maintain the performance of that behavior under the proper circumstances.

Modeling is an important means of acquiring new behavior patterns, is effective in strengthening or weakening inhibitions, and observing a model often serves as an S^D to perform previously learned behavior. Modeling is important in learning speech, athletic skills, social skills and other complex behaviors. Live modeling is thought to be particularly powerful in institutional settings such as schools, prisons, and mental hospitals. Modeling helps teach the *know how* of a behavior, but doesn't necessarily mean that the behavior will be performed by the observers, unless a contingency is involved, either observed or in real life for the new learner. The combination of modeling for teaching how to perform a new behavior, together with positive reinforcement for actually performing the behavior, is very powerful.

Classical conditioning   By now some of you who may have taken a general psychology course somewhere along the way may be saying something like "I remember hearing about some Russian guy who did strange things to dogs. Where does all that come in?"

Well, since you asked, this is as good a place as any for it to come in. Let me try to refresh your memory. Does the name Pavlov ring a bell? Earlier we talked about B. F. Skinner as sort of being the father of a kind of learning usually called operant conditioning. In the same way Ivan Pavlov can be thought of as the father of another kind of learning usually called *classical conditioning*, but sometimes referred to as *respondent conditioning* or simply *Pavlovian conditioning*.

In his classic experiment Pavlov is said to have conditioned a dog to salivate at the sound of a bell. Before he started his experiment, the bell was quite neutral. In other words the bell had no effect on the dog, at least as far as salivation was concerned. Pavlov could ring the bell all he wanted. The dog might have done a lot of other things, but did not salivate. On the other hand Pavlov knew that if he put meat powder in the dog's mouth the dog certainly would start salivating. So Pavlov tried ringing the bell (which, in Pavlovian terminology, was called a neutral stimulus) followed immediately by putting the meat powder (called an unconditioned or unconditional stimulus) in the dog's mouth, which resulted in the unconditioned salivation. After doing this for a while Pavlov found that if he just rang the bell, even without the meat powder following it, the dog would still salivate, at least for a while. So after all this happens, the bell (formerly known as a neutral stimulus) gets its name changed to *conditioned* or *conditional* stimulus (depends on which translation of Pavlov you read). That is, it works as a stimulus to elicit, or bring about, salivation as long as, or under the condition that, every so often it is followed with our old reliable unconditioned meat powder, to sort of recharge the connection. If we keep going on and on with just the bell and no meat powder, eventually we have a form of extinction take place and we are back where we started, with the bell ringing becoming pretty much a neutral stimulus again. All bell and no saliva.

Pavlov and his followers conducted many more experiments on dogs and other animals and discovered quite a bit about the process of learning. Others have taken these findings and have developed effective treatments for a variety of human behavior problems.

While classical conditioning certainly is important, perhaps the area of behavior modification where we see classical conditioning used the most is in the treatment of maladaptive emotional behaviors such as phobias. Many phobic and other emotional behavior problems have been shown to develop through classical conditioning and also to be effectively treated through behavior therapy techniques based on classical conditioning principles. But this is not generally thought of as a part of ABA and we won't go into all that now. If you are interested in reading more about this, many of the writings of Joseph Wolpe (e.g. Wolpe and Wolpe 1988) would be a good place to start.

Rule-governed behavior   Sometimes you may hear the term *rule-governed behavior*. Distinctions are made between *contingency-shaped behavior*, which we've already talked about a lot, and rule-governed behavior. I hope you remember that contingency-shaped behavior involves *real* consequences (reinforcers, punishers, etc.). Rule-governed behavior refers to situations in which some individuals respond well to verbal directions to do this or to do that, often with a consequence either clearly stated or implied, but that may not be actually experienced first hand. "Eat your vegetables and you'll grow up to be big and strong." "If you hit your sister again you can't watch TV tonight." "Don't touch that hot stove" ("or you'll burn yourself" as an unspoken implied consequence). "Do your homework" ("and someday you'll get a good job," again often implied as a long-delayed consequence). In these situations and others like them, the contingencies don't usually happen in the student's real life, but the student behaves pretty much as if they did. Some people are much more responsive than others to rules. Although there certainly are exceptions, children with ASDs are thought to adhere more rigidly to learned rules than the general population. On the other hand people with ADHD are thought to be less influenced by rules, and more often have to learn things the hard way (that is, experience the consequences themselves, so we say more of their behavior is contingency shaped). If you like analogies, contingency shaped is to rule governed as experiencing something yourself is to being told about something. Since learning through rules and modeling both involve behavior changes without directly experiencing the behavioral consequences, some might say we are talking about different aspects of the same learning process.

Covert conditioning   There is another kind of learning called *covert conditioning* which involves having the individual imagine the behavior to be influenced and then imagining an appropriate consequence to change that behavior. It is beyond the scope of this book to discuss covert conditioning here. There are some published reports that have found covert conditioning procedures to be helpful with some autistic students at The Groden Center in Providence, Rhode Island (e.g. Groden 1993), so it is possible that if you are reading this you have heard the term covert conditioning. There are a lot of similarities between covert conditioning, modeling, and rule-governed behavior.

Learning in real-life situations is usually more complicated than it appears in these simplified illustrations. Learning, unlearning, and relearning are constantly taking place. Everything we do in the presence of others can have some effect on their behavior. But the processes through which learning occurs are the same for everyone, and techniques based on these principles can be adjusted to fit any situation.

Part 2

PUTTING IT ALL TOGETHER

Chapter 6

WHAT IS A BEHAVIOR ANALYSIS?

Ten steps to bring it all together

One of the greatest advantages of using a behavioral approach to helping with human problems is that it includes methods for objectively evaluating the procedures used to treat the problems. We can then make our treatment decisions based on scientific methods of assessment that use objective evidence and actual data rather than just relying on subjective opinions and wishful thinking. With this approach the treatments can be continued, adjusted, or discontinued and replaced based on the evidence of objective data.

When someone does something unusual, it is not at all unusual to have someone else ask "What makes someone do something like that?"— especially if the person asking happens to know that you are a psychologist. Seems like a natural question to ask, but the truth is that there is no one answer to that question that fits all cases. The same behaviors may be performed by different people for different reasons, different behaviors may be performed by different people for the same reasons, and the same person may perform the same behavior at different times for different reasons. Pretty confusing, isn't it?

So what can we do to try to understand what's really going on and what can be done about it? In treating a problem from a behavioral point of view, the first thing to do is what is commonly called a *behavior analysis*. This is simply a method of sizing up the problem situation and planning what to do about it.

The terms *functional analysis* and *functional behavioral assessment* are often used in talking about ways of looking at and sizing up behavior problems. They have to do with identifying the variables of which behavior is a function, whatever that means. The key word in these and similar terms is *functional*. What we are trying to figure out here is what function, or purpose, the behavior serves. What does it accomplish? How does it pay off? How does the behavior operate to increase the child's general level of reinforcement? Does the behavior function to avoid or escape from something aversive, or does the behavior result in positive reinforcement of some sort? If our goal is to replace a maladaptive behavior with more adaptive behavior, it is not as important to figure out what made the troublesome behavior happen in the first place (which could have been years ago) as it is to figure out what's keeping the behavior going now ("What's in it for Jane?"). What function does the behavior serve now? For example, it is common to see children with communication deficits learn that physically intrusive behaviors of some sort or another can function to get the attention of others.

Functional analysis   *Functional analysis* refers to a more science-based approach that involves keeping most factors or variables unchanged (or constant) while intentionally changing other factors (As and Cs) that might influence the target behavior (B). By keeping track of what changes, if any, do occur in the target behavior we can come to a more objective understanding of how certain behaviors may or may not be influenced by changes in the environment.

Functional behavioral assessment (FBA)   *Functional behavioral assessment* (*FBA*) is generally a broader term in that a functional behavioral assessment may include a functional analysis, but also includes other types of information gathering such as reviewing existing records and interviewing adults who know the child well. The goal is still to achieve an understanding of the relationship between the child's behavior and various factors that may influence the behavior.

There are a number of approaches to behavioral assessment that are useful for sizing up problems, planning what to do, and evaluating the plan's effectiveness. Information for assessments is commonly gathered by using a variety of methods including direct observation, obtaining dependable information from individuals who know the child well, and occasionally from direct interviews with the child. Assessment may include the use of assessment forms and behavior rating scales completed by the parents and teachers. Often the decisions about what behaviors to target are made after talking with parents and teachers, followed by informal observations to confirm or refine first impressions. Direct observations by trained observers, who know what to look for and how to best record what they observe, usually is the major component of a good behavioral assessment.

As I mentioned earlier, while most initial referrals don't provide sufficient information to develop a behavior treatment plan, they should at least be helpful to give us some pretty good ideas of where to start. By talking with the individual making the referral, the parents, the teachers and others who have day-in and day-out ongoing knowledge of the child, we can usually get a better idea of what the problem behaviors are. Asking the caregivers to complete more lengthy structured questionnaires about the child's behavior can help guide informants toward giving us more useful information. This process can also help them to learn to think of these things from a more behavioral perspective, sort of like learning to see things from someone else's point of view, or to think in a second language besides English.

An old but still useful technique for getting a quick idea of what is going on during a classroom observation is based on our ABCs. Since observers tend to take notes of whatever they see happening anyway, it can be helpful to make three columns on a sheet of paper, with headings A (for antecedents), B (for behaviors), and C (for consequences). As the observer writes a running narrative of what is happening across the page, the events can be almost automatically sorted into the As, Bs and Cs.

Time	A	B	C
9:46	Teacher turns her back to the class	Dick throws a paper airplane	Class laughs
9:47	Teacher turns around	Dick resumes copying from blackboard	——

This method has been a great help in bridging the gap between referral reasons that are too subjective or incomplete to be all that useful and more detailed and specific data-gathering observational techniques.

There are numerous systems for conducting a behavior analysis. The ten-step method presented here is based on the system previously recommended by Cautela and Kearney (1986, 1990) as a means of analyzing and treating problems from a behavioral perspective.

Step 1. Operationalize the target behavior

The first step is to operationalize the problem. That means spell it out. Saying Dick is aggressive or Jane has a poor self-image doesn't tell us anything very useful. Why do we say Dick is aggressive? Maybe it's because he throws things at his teacher. Well, then, that's what we are interested in—Dick's *throwing* behavior. The behaviors to be modified should be specified or *operationalized* as objectively as possible. Saying that Dick is disruptive in class doesn't tell us very much. Saying Dick hits the girl who sits in front of him over the head with a book every time she turns around tells us a lot more.

A common reason for referral is childhood aggression. But what does that mean, and how do we get to a referral for aggression? Well, first Dick usually does something that someone in authority doesn't like. Or maybe Jane doesn't do something and the person in authority doesn't like that either. That might be called passive aggression.

Anyway, suppose, for example, Dick draws a lot of pictures of weapons dripping blood and dismembered bodies in class. Or Jane tells a classmate that she will "get her" for playing with someone else at recess. Or a third student stays seated in his chair but growls when others approach him closely. Rather than just repeating the specific objective behaviors of concern, many adults might interpret these events as *aggression*, and simply report the child as being aggressive, perhaps thinking that they have performed a clear and helpful service by taking their objective observations to another level, a level of interpretation and assigning a presumed cause of the behavior. (Sometimes we are better off asking Dick's classmates what he does that bothers people. We are usually more likely to get a straight answer from children about many of these things.)

So now we have Dr. Lynch, the psychologist, reviewing the referral, reading that Dick is aggressive. But Dr. Lynch never saw Dick in action and at this point has no other source of information or context to use to help interpret this information. Because of her own previous experiences and expectations of the term *aggressive*, Dr. Lynch has thoughts and memories of other students physically beating other children and makes the (false) assumption that Dick is behaving the same way. So by going from an objective observation to a subjective label, then back to another presumed objective view about what a student is up to, we have seriously miscommunicated the truth of the matter and thereby set the stage for all sorts of additional problems. It would have been much easier in the first place to just keep matters at the objective observation level. Things got all mixed up once they got to that subjective hypothetical construct label level.

Take a great work of English literature, say one of Shakespeare's poems. Translate that into a foreign language, even a relatively well-known language like French. Then have someone else who never read the poem translate it from French back into English. How much like the original poem is this second-order translation likely to be? Do you think you'd get the message Shakespeare originally intended to communicate? I suspect old Bill would be turning over in his grave if he ever saw what we ended up with.

Another common referral reason, poor self-image or low self-esteem, also isn't very useful and doesn't tell us that much either. What does Jane do or not do that gets us to say that she has a poor self-image? Does she make a lot of comments in which she seems to be always finding fault with herself? Does she act passively when classmates try to take advantage of her? That's what we need to know and what we need to work on changing.

Behavioral objective Many behavioral treatment plans are based on the use of *behavioral objectives* to set goals to guide our interventions and to evaluate how well the interventions are working. Some experts have described behavioral objectives as a specification of learning in terms of observable, measurable behavior. More simply, behavioral objectives are a statement of the behaviors that we want Jane to perform. What are our objectives in terms of the behavioral changes we want Jane to achieve? Good behavioral objectives usually have five components to them:

1. who (will perform the behavior)

2. the behavior

3. the result (the product or performance)

4. the conditions (e.g. in the dining hall, given a list of 20 words, etc.)

5. the criteria (four out of five times, 90% accuracy).

An example might be something like "Dick will correctly spell nine out of ten words taken from Chapter 6 of the fourth-grade spelling book."

Step 2. Find the baseline

The second step is to get a *baseline*, which means finding out how often the child performs the target behavior under typical circumstances. This is usually done by having an observer sit in a classroom for a week or so watching Dick and his interaction with the environment, and counting the behaviors of interest. Teachers can sometimes collect baseline data themselves, as can aides or even students in the class.

The purpose of a baseline is to assist us in monitoring the target behavior. Once we have a baseline we should then be able to tell rather quickly if our treatment is making things better, worse, or not having any effect at all simply by checking to see if there is a decrease, increase, or no change in the frequency of the target behavior. Remember back in Chapter 2 we talked about the importance of frequency and rates of behavior? These numbers we come up with are referred to as *data*, and they are extremely useful in making decisions based more on factual evidence than on subjective opinions. It is typical to gather baseline data for a week or two before beginning an intervention. This allows us to get a more representative and stable sample of the target behavior without treatment, so that once we try to do something to improve the behavior we can make a more informed data-based decision about whether what we're trying is really helping or not. This also enables us to make future adjustments to the program based on real evidence.

It is common for the first few days of collecting baseline information to be a bit abnormal simply because of the presence of another adult in the classroom, which can be a big change to the environment. If a new person comes into the classroom to do the observing, that person should not get involved in classroom activities and should try to minimize interacting with the children. Essentially the observer should, as much as reasonably possible, try to hide in a corner with a good view. This is to have as little effect as possible on the classroom environment and the target behaviors.

Once treatment begins, the same methods that were used for gathering data during the pretreatment baseline period are usually continued to aid in monitoring progress and evaluating the effectiveness of the treatment we are using. Even when treatment is complete, occasional follow-up data gathering can be helpful in some cases to watch for signs of relapse.

When gathering baseline data we usually don't have to be constantly watching and counting all behaviors that occur. We are essentially collecting a sample of behavior, in much the same way that opinion pollsters might ask a sample of voters which candidate they favor in the next election. When the sampling is done properly, we can usually get a good idea of what the big picture looks like. In dealing with many school-based behavior problems, samples of 30–60 minutes of the school day can be effective, but we often would need to vary the time from day to day to get a representation of the whole picture.

Event sampling   There are two general types of behavior sampling that are commonly used. The first, which is called *event sampling*, is a count of the frequency or the number of occurrences of the target behavior within a set period of time. That is, how many times does the behavior happen every minute, every ten minutes, every hour, or whatever. Event sampling is useful in counting discrete behaviors with clear beginnings and endings (e.g. the number of times Dick gets up to sharpen his pencil or the number of animals Jane can name in 15 seconds) and is usually recorded by some type of tally count (e.g. $\cancel{||||}$, $//$). Sometimes the amount of time it takes to do something is counted using event sampling: for example, the amount of time it takes Jane to run around the track in gym class or the total amount of time that Dick is in (or out) of his chair during silent reading.

Time sampling   The second type of sampling is called *time sampling*. Time sampling has to do with whether or not a behavior is present or absent at certain points in time and is useful with behaviors that are not so discrete and are more continuous or difficult to count. Making nonsensical vocal noises or talking with a classmate would be examples of behaviors that probably would be counted by time sampling, since it would be difficult to decide when one instance of a behavior ends and the next one begins. In time sampling, a short uniform time interval unit is selected, perhaps in the range of 10–30 seconds. If the behavior occurs at all during that period, whether just for one second or for all 30 seconds, it is recorded as present. A useful rule of thumb is that if a behavior occurs less than once per 15-minute time period, we should try to find a way to use event sampling.

Duration   Once a behavior or a pattern or sequence of behaviors gets started, the length of time the behavior goes on is called the *duration* of the behavior. Changes in duration are one of the ways we can spot improvement in behavior. If Jane is still having about five tantrums a day, but now the typical duration of her tantrums is four minutes instead of the previous ten minutes, that's improvement.

Although there are many different recording systems that can be used, it is often most useful to develop an individualized system for the unique situation. Teachers and parents may use wrist counters like those worn by golfers or use bead counters they can wear on their belts, whereas other observers may have a recording sheet with a shorthand code to enter appropriate symbols (e.g. O = no problem, S = out of seat, H = hitting, Y = yelling, etc.).

The data collected through these observations are usually presented by some sort of visual display, such as graph paper, to enable a quick check as to how the rate of behavior is changing over time. In some programs you might see a funny-looking kind of graph paper sometimes called a *standard celeration chart*, which is used in a very specialized and effective approach to teaching known as *precision teaching*, which we'll talk more about later. While these charts can be very helpful when you know how to use and read them, it does take some specialized training, but even elementary-age school children can learn to use these charts to keep track of their own behavior.

Step 3. Identify the antecedents

The next step is to try to pin down the antecedents of the target behavior. Is there anything that consistently happens right before the target behavior occurs? For example, maybe his teacher always turns her back to the class to write on the blackboard just before Dick throws something at her. Identifying antecedents has to do with those SDs and EOs we talked about way back in Chapter 3. Remember them?

Latency   In trying to identify the antecedents of a behavior or a sequence of behaviors, we should keep in mind the notion of *latency*. Latency refers to the length of time between the antecedent and the behavior. If the teacher tells Dick to put away his crayons and take out his reading book, the time it takes him to get started is the latency. In many instances the latency is very brief, but can be more noticeable. Finding the antecedents of a behavior is usually relatively difficult and, although quite helpful, not always absolutely necessary.

It is also important to know where and when the target behavior occurs most often and least often. These can be thought of as special kinds of antecedents.

Step 4. Note the place

Where does the target behavior occur? What is the most common location for the behavior? Perhaps at school but rarely at home. Perhaps during silent reading but not during music. Perhaps in the lunch room and out at recess, but never in the classroom. By identifying specific locations we can often get clues to the S^Ds that have strong effects on target behaviors.

Perhaps the events going on in those locations are what is important. Perhaps it is something about the physical characteristics such as color, lighting, noise, temperature, or objects or persons in the room that has the greatest influence on behavior.

It is also important to find out where the behavior does not occur, or occurs at a relatively low rate. Useful clues may be found that suggest changes that can be brought into the high frequency setting to help reduce the frequency of the target behavior. On the other hand we might be doing a behavior analysis of a behavior we want to strengthen or increase. Then of course we use this information to arrange the environment to make Dick more likely to engage in the target behavior.

Step 5. Note the time

Time is important primarily because knowing the time can give us clues to what might routinely be going on at the time the target behavior occurs. Is it just before lunch and Jane is hungry? Is it early in the day and certain medications may have just been taken?

As with location, or *where*, time has to do with the *when* question and is helpful for finding out what is or is not going on at high and low frequency times. But we shouldn't limit our investigations to what is going on in the external environment. To paraphrase Skinner, "The environment doesn't end at the skin," so what's happening inside our bodies is also important to consider. Perhaps it's 11:30 and Dick is very hungry. As we've all experienced first hand, hunger can influence behavior.

Perhaps a medication has worn off, or perhaps it's 14:00 and Jane is quite fatigued after a long day at school, or it's 22:00 and she hasn't gotten to bed yet.

Scatter plot   We recently looked at using tally marks as a way of keeping count of the frequency of a target behavior. An even better way in many cases is to use some variation of what is called a *scatter plot*. A scatter plot is a frequency recording method that helps determine when the target behavior happens most and happens least. This could be as simple as using a piece of paper with time periods written in the left margin. We would then just tally the target behaviors in the space next to the appropriate time period.

Suppose we're trying to keep track of how often Dick touches his classmates. Part of a simple scatter plot might look like this:

10:00–10:15 //

10:16–10:30 /

10:31–10:45 ~~////~~ ///

10:46–11:00 //

From this data we know that Dick touched classmates 13 times during this hour. But we can also see that eight of the touches, more than half, were in the 10:31–10:45 time period. When we check Dick's schedule we see that this was the time of morning recess break. This tells us that some potentially important factors changed in Dick's environment, including Dick's location (or place), the activity, and the adult supervision. These are all useful bits of information to consider as we continue on with our behavior analysis.

To help organize this data many people find it helpful to use graph paper or to design forms to record the data in various grids on the paper. The actual design of these forms can be quite different, depending on the needs of the unique situation.

Step 6. Identify the consequences

Even more important than the antecedents are the consequences of the behavior, especially what happens immediately after the behavior. Maybe after Dick throws an object in class the teacher turns red and screams at the class, which Dick thinks is a really funny sight.

So now we have a lot more useful information about what is going on than simply being told that Dick is aggressive. We know that every time the teacher turns her back to write on the board, Dick throws something at her and she turns red and screams at the class. Now this is much more helpful than hearing someone just labeling Dick as an aggressive child. This series of antecedents, behaviors, and consequences is what we go to work on, not the label aggressive.

It is important to remember that in real-life situations the reinforcers that shape, strengthen, and maintain target behaviors rarely occur after every instance of that behavior. Remember earlier we talked about intermittent reinforcement schedules? Intermittent reinforcement schedules are extremely common in real life, so we usually need to observe several instances of a behavior to get a good idea about what reinforcers are involved.

Step 7. Identify the positive reinforcers and aversive stimuli

The next step is to determine what is reinforcing and what is aversive to Dick so that this can be taken into account in planning whatever programs we develop. There are a number of ways in which this can be done. The simplest of course is to just ask Dick what he likes and doesn't like. There is a form called the *Reinforcement Survey Schedule* which is very useful with high school age students and adults for this purpose. There are also *Children's Reinforcement Survey Schedules* for elementary school age children. These and many other useful forms for working with children can be found in a book called *Forms for Behavior Analysis with Children* by Cautela, Cautela and Esonis (1983). We can also ask Dick's caretakers and others who know him well for ideas. There are reinforcement survey schedules for parents to fill out, too, about their children's likes and dislikes.

Premack Principle   Another way of determining reinforcers is simply to observe Dick to see what kinds of things he chooses to do in a free choice situation when given a choice of a variety of possibilities. In other words, in determining reinforcers, whichever of two things an individual does more often when given a choice can often be used as a reinforcer for the other. Actually, as a general rule of thumb, the opportunity to perform behaviors that one ordinarily engages in quite a bit will usually function or work as a reinforcer for a less frequent behavior. For example, if the only way a chain smoker who didn't like working on his income taxes could smoke was to work on the taxes for a while, pretty soon the taxes would be finished. Or how about what is sometimes called *Grandma's Law*? Grandma may tell Jane, "You don't get your apple pie until you eat your vegetables." Using higher probability behaviors to reinforce lower probability behaviors is called the *Premack Principle*. Left to herself Jane would talk to her friends on the telephone rather than do her homework. So the privilege of using the telephone could be made contingent or dependent upon doing X amount of homework first. When done carefully, access to things and activities with which a child has a seemingly excessive interest or fascination can be used to reinforce other behavior.

General level of reinforcement (GLR)   In general, a reinforcer is likely to be more powerful if someone has not been receiving much reinforcement of any sort lately. On the other hand if the individual has been receiving a lot of reinforcement, a given reinforcer is likely to be less powerful. This overall state of reinforcement is sometimes referred to as the *general level of reinforcement.*

Remember, reinforcers can come in the form of something tangible like a goodie to eat, or something intangible like a smile from someone we like. But the same things are not reinforcing for everybody and something that is a reinforcer for someone at one time in one situation may not be reinforcing at a different time or in a different situation. Even if you love chicken salad sandwiches, how hard would you work for one right after eating Thanksgiving dinner?

Of course these methods can be helpful to get ideas of where to start in identifying reinforcers. But the only way to know for sure is to be experimental, try the likely reinforcers out, and see what happens to the behavior.

Reinforcement sampling   Sometimes a procedure called *reinforcement sampling* is used to introduce potential new reinforcers. Various possible reinforcers are offered noncontingently, that is, with no strings attached. In other words we don't have to do anything special to get them; they are free (at first). We've all been offered free samples of new food products in supermarkets and we've received free samples of new products in the mail to get us to try a new product and perhaps buy more of the product later. This is a form of reinforcement sampling, same idea.

Variations of many of the methods used for identifying positive reinforcers can also be used to identify aversive stimuli. Since we want to emphasize the positive, however, we won't be going into that right now.

In thinking about reinforcers don't forget that a particularly important kind of reinforcement that we mentioned in Chapter 4 is *social reinforcement,* which comes in the form of attention from others. Human beings are social beings and attention can be a very powerful reinforcer. The more important the person giving the attention is to the person receiving the reinforcer, the more powerful the attention usually is. Attention can come in many forms: a smile, a word, a physical touch, a meeting of the eyes. For some individuals with unusual backgrounds, even a scolding, a punch, or a kick can be reinforcing. Sadly, for many individuals with ASDs, social reinforcement is not as effective as it is with most people.

Step 8. Plan and implement the program

We're now at the point in our behavior analysis where we've got to decide what to do about the target behavior. We must develop a program and give it a try. We look over the information we've gathered so far. We use our operationalized behaviors to specify behavioral objectives as goals to work on. The easiest solution in the case of Dick's throwing objects in class of course would be to eliminate the S^D, the discriminative stimulus, which in this hypothetical case was the teacher turning her back to write on the board, but this is not always possible. While stimulus control procedures can be very helpful, the meat and potatoes of most ABA programs will probably involve some combination of a way to reinforce the behaviors we want to increase while using extinction to weaken undesirable behaviors.

Step 9. Monitor the program

Once a program is designed for the unique child in his or her unique situation the plan is put into operation, but that is not the end of it. We have to keep a close watch on what happens next. We continue to observe and record data so that we have an ongoing record of what is happening, to help us to better understand any changes since baseline. This is like continuing an ongoing baseline. Testing the effect of an intervention is often called *probing*, or conducting a *probe*. Sometimes after a treatment has been in place for a period of time, even if there is an encouraging change in the target behavior and the treatment appears to be helping, the intervention is intentionally discontinued for a limited period of time. This temporarily returns the situation to the original baseline conditions. If the target behavior returns to baseline levels, this is considered to be evidence that the treatment intervention was in fact responsible for the improved behavior and the intervention is reinstated. This whole process is sometimes referred to as an A–B–A–B *reversal design*, with A representing the pretreatment baseline conditions and B representing the addition of a particular treatment. So A–B–A–B represents baseline–treatment–baseline (again)–treatment (again).

Another common way to monitor an intervention plan is by using what is called a *multiple baseline* approach. In multiple baseline the treatment stays in place once it is implemented (assuming an acceptable behavior change occurs), but the treatment is expanded in sequential steps as it is applied to address additional behaviors one at a time. Multiple baseline is particularly useful when it is difficult or highly undesirable to reverse the behaviors, or it is not practical to reverse treatment to allow a problem behavior to temporarily return.

Step 10. Evaluate and adjust the program

As we monitor the program and continue to gather ongoing data we need to make a judgment about the changes, if any, that are taking place in Dick's behavior. If the program isn't working, then we have to adjust the program until it does. This may require going over some of the earlier steps again. This is where accountability comes in. We don't want to waste everyone's time and efforts doing things that aren't helping. By examining and analyzing what's going on by using scientific evidence-based methods, we can better find what is and isn't working, and then make better decisions for changes based on science rather than on hunches. An ABA approach allows for trials of numerous interventions, but evaluates them all fairly, impartially, and scientifically. It certainly is not a one-size-fits-all approach as is sometimes seen with some other approaches.

When evaluating behavior change programs we should not expect overnight miracles. Bad habits usually don't develop overnight and neither do good habits. Like many bad habits, many of the maladaptive behaviors that we are trying to change have had months if not years of reinforcement, and it is reasonable to expect that it will take some length of time to bring about satisfactory changes. We should, however, watch for and be encouraged by trends and improvements in the wanted direction, and take this as evidence that we are on the right track and be patient.

Changes in patterns of behavior rarely take place right away and these changes usually do not take place smoothly. If Dick never used to finish his class reading assignment and now is finishing it two days each week, that is probably an encouraging improvement. It's not where we want to end up, but we're clearly moving in the right direction. Along the way Dick is likely to take a few steps backwards. After getting up to three days per week he might temporarily slip back to two days before progressing on to four days. When these slip-backs occur, this is not a reason to be surprised and is certainly not a reason to immediately throw out the program. Be patient, give it a bit more time, and see what happens. Maybe minor adjustments, if anything, are all that are needed to get the ball rolling again.

A student once came up with the following sentence to help remember these ten steps of a behavior analysis:

Our	Operationalize (the target behavior)
Behavior	Baseline
Analysts	Antecedents
Place	Place
The	Time
Child	Consequences
In	Identify (positive reinforcers and aversive stimuli)

Prudently	Plan (and implement a program)
Monitored	Monitor (the program)
Environments	Evaluate (and adjust the program)

Maybe it will help you remember these steps too!

When we began this chapter someone had said that Dick was being aggressive. But throughout this whole process the label *aggressive* hasn't been useful to us at all. This is one of the reasons why we don't use labels such as neurotic, psychotic, or emotionally disturbed. People don't fit smoothly into any of these categories and, even if they did, it wouldn't make any difference in how we try to help them, so labels are not particularly useful (but sometimes are needed for bureaucratic purposes). A formal medical diagnosis can of course be useful in treating medical conditions and when medications may be prescribed, but are generally less useful when we're using educational and other environmental treatments to improve behavior. Then it's much more helpful to know the As, Bs and Cs of the target behaviors.

I certainly wouldn't expect most parents and teachers to be gathering all this information and conducting a behavior analysis on their own. But now you know some of the important questions you may be asked to help answer, and why.

Chapter 7

WHAT DO WE DO NEXT?

So far we have been talking mostly about general laws and principles and a general method for applying them. Now we need to talk about specific applications of these behavioral laws and principles. In other words, we need to talk about what we actually can go out and do if we want to change the way someone behaves.

As we begin, an important point to remember is that whether we are using reinforcers to strengthen behavior, or aversive consequences to weaken behavior, it is important that these consequences immediately follow the target behavior, or we risk reinforcing or punishing the wrong behavior. Also, keep in mind that these basic learning operations are often used in combinations with each other to help learning take place more effectively.

Now here are some of the more common applications of behavior analysis that you are likely to encounter in the world of ABA.

Shaping   When we want to strengthen a new behavior, we often don't have the time to wait for it to occur on its own so we can reinforce it. Most goal or target behaviors occur rarely, if at all, if they are not reinforced in some way. They may not yet be in the child's behavioral repertoire. In some cases we would be waiting forever for the behaviors to occur. If we are trying to teach Jane to swim, it's not very likely that some fine day she's just going to jump in the water and start right off doing the crawl stroke for the first time, giving us the chance to reinforce her swimming. So it is often necessary to *shape* the desired behavior. By *shaping* we mean reinforcing successive approximations of the desired behavior as the behaviors become more and more like the target behavior that we want to end up with.

Shaping is essentially using a combination of positive reinforcement and extinction: positive reinforcement to strengthen the behavior in the intended direction, while extinguishing behavior in the unwanted or no longer wanted direction. We keep replacing behavior that we recently reinforced with new, improved, closer to the goal behavior. For example, if we want Dick, who seems to be always running around, to sit in his seat, we might have to begin by reinforcing him for coming closer and closer to his seat, eventually touching the seat, until finally we have him sitting down. It is important to remember not to reinforce him for any behavior further from the desired behavior than has already been reinforced. Also, he should only be reinforced for closer approximations of the desired behavior and usually not for the same behavior twice, until we reach the behavior we want. For example, if we have already reinforced Dick for being three feet from his desk, we should not reinforce him for being four feet away or even for staying at three feet. We should wait until he approaches closer than three feet and then reinforce him immediately.

Sometimes people are hesitant to act when a wanted behavior finally shows up. They may be worried about messing things up and upsetting the balance. They think they should hold their breaths and let sleeping dogs lie, and just hope for the best. But this is really the golden opportunity to *catch them being good*.

If we think about it, the Hot and Cold game that we sometimes play with children is actually based on a form of shaping. When we tell Jane that she is getting warmer when she gets closer to a hidden prize we are using positive reinforcement to shape her closer and closer to the target. Or think of a sculptor chiseling a block of marble closer and closer to a statue of Abraham Lincoln. The sculptor's sculpting is reinforced as the marble begins to look more and more like old Abe.

Another way in which shaping could be used is in teaching Jane to read on the fourth-grade level. Jane must begin by learning the alphabet, various words, reading on a first-grade level and so on up each step, getting closer and closer to the final goal. But Jane should be reinforced as she takes each successively closer step. Algebra is similarly learned through a series of steps over several years: first learning the names of the numbers and then counting, later simple arithmetic, and eventually algebra. Social behavior, such as cooperative play, might be shaped by reinforcing children first for playing in closer proximity to each other, next for talking to each other, and then for engaging in increasingly involved interactive play.

In using shaping we often vary the size of the step needed for reinforcement. Our goal, however, is to keep things moving in the right direction as we selectively reinforce behaviors which more and more closely resemble the target behavior.

Response differentiation   Related to shaping is a procedure referred to as *response differentiation*. Sometimes a behavior does occur from time to time, but not usually in a form up to acceptable standards. With response differentiation only those instances of the behavior that do meet acceptable standards are reinforced. For example, these differences in behavior could have to do with various qualities of the behaviors such as strength and duration, or they might have to do with the rate or speed at which the behavior is performed. This helps the student to learn to discriminate what forms or standards of behavior are acceptable and what are not. A teacher might use response differentiation to help a student learn to use legible penmanship more consistently, or a speech therapist might use response differentiation to teach a student to consistently speak more clearly. Performances of behaviors that acceptably resemble the goals are reinforced while sloppy attempts are extinguished.

Behavioral drift   Understanding shaping and response differentiation should make it easier to understand *behavioral drift*. We don't always perform behaviors the same way each and every time we do them. After all, we're not robots, are we? Whether it's taking a foul shot in basketball, playing a song on a piano, or greeting an acquaintance we have just run into, there are often small, sometimes larger and more noticeable differences in our behavior. We might have a typical or *average* way of doing something, but once in a while we do it a little better and other times we do it a little worse, more this way or more that way. Factors that remain consistent in the environment work to keep the form or topography of the behavior close to that typical performance most of the time. When some of these controlling factors are removed or lose their effectiveness, other factors may start having greater influence and the behavior starts to deviate even more from the previously typical behavior. This process is sometimes called *behavioral drift*. Physicists use the term *entropy* to describe the tendency of the amount of disorder in a system to increase over time if things are left to themselves. Same idea.

In the natural environment, where the effective feedback and contingencies are less consistent, we are more often taking our chances with random, inconsistent antecedents and consequences, so even well-trained and practiced behavior patterns have a tendency to get sloppy if we're not careful. To avoid excessive drift we still need occasional positive reinforcement to keep us on the right track, sort of like resetting a fine watch when it starts to lose time.

In a prosthetic or therapeutic environment we might employ response differentiation (OK, go back and look up *response differentiation* if you need to) by using extinction to weaken these tendencies to drift, while using positive reinforcement to strengthen the more precise performance that we hope to encourage. Think of little tug boats gently nudging a big ocean liner on its way toward the dock in the harbor, as they try to keep the ship on a precise, straight and narrow course, while the wind and currents work to turn the ship from its course. Perhaps positive feedback from a music teacher or a skating coach works as the positive reinforcement that helps make a top-level performance become a more consistent habit.

On the other hand we might do just the opposite and use this tendency toward behavioral drift to our advantage. We might use shaping to strengthen the deviations that we consider to be improvements, while we use extinction to lessen the likelihood that the more typical performance reoccurs. We try to move on and leave old habits behind.

One example of behavioral drift that we've probably all experienced has to do with our handwriting. Back in the early grades when teachers put a lot of emphasis on neatness and letter formation, many of us probably routinely wrote more legibly than we do today, particularly if our fine-motor coordination was developing well. Taking fast lecture notes in high school and college is a great way to mess up your handwriting. In addition, few people are correcting us for sloppy handwriting these days.

The notion of drift can apply to larger situations such as a classroom too. Maybe Ms. Smith's class has a very consistent and well-practiced routine for coming back from recess and getting right to work on an extra silent reading period. She has worked hard all fall to get this routine established and it makes her feel happy to see her students follow it so well.

Toward the end of November Ms. Smith goes out on maternity leave and Ms. Jones comes in as a long-term substitute teacher for the class. While Ms. Jones is a fine teacher, she doesn't know anything about the "from recess right to silent reading" policy. For the first few days the class still follows the old routine out of habit, but before long one or two of the children may dawdle and chat a little longer before getting down to work. Ms. Smith isn't there to guide them back on the straight and narrow, and to Ms. Jones it's no big deal. She thinks of this time as sort of a free period for students to use as they want (within reason), so she doesn't intervene one way or the other. Soon we have four or five students drifting away from Ms. Smith's routine and, as I'm sure you can imagine, before long there are only a handful of students still making much of an effort to do silent reading.

Behavioral sociologists would say that behavioral drift occurs on much larger scales too. It often happens to the culture of a school or other organizations and even to the culture of the larger society. This process contributes to changes in cultural practices and values over time, but this is a topic for another time and place.

In some situations behaviors tend to drift more than in other situations.

Behavioral momentum   Behavior that has received a lot of reinforcement on intermittent reinforcement schedules is sometimes quite resistant to change, even when the reinforcement is decreased or stopped. The degree of resistance to change is thought of as the behavior's *response strength* and the tendency of the behavior to just keep going on, unless something else happens to change it, is called *behavioral momentum*. In science class you might have learned about what physicists call *inertia*. That is, the tendency of an object to keep moving on the same way it has been moving (or just staying still if it hasn't been moving) until some new force acts on the object. Behavioral momentum is the same idea.

Procedures based on behavioral momentum can sometimes be helpful in dealing with noncompliance situations. (That is, not doing what you are told to do.) Suppose Dick won't take out the trash when we ask him to. But we know that there are many things that he will do. So next time we try to get some behavioral momentum built up before we tell him to take out the trash. We might accomplish this by using what some experts refer to as an *antecedent high-probability command sequence*. In plain English, we can set this up by first instructing Dick to do several of the reinforcing activities that we know he is very likely to do. We might start by asking Dick to show us his new toy space ship that he doesn't seem to be able to put down. Then we might tell Dick to go turn on the TV, then go out to the car and bring in the package of cookies we left there so we can have a snack, and so on. Once we've built up the behavioral momentum and Dick is moving along complying with our directions (and receiving a lot of reinforcement for complying), we again tell Dick to take out the trash. Research has shown that this method really does increase our chances of getting compliance. It doesn't work all the time, but certainly can be worth a try.

In classroom situations teachers can help get the day off to a good start by beginning the day with well-liked activities. Once things are under way the less enjoyable work can be done, then, toward the end of the day, finish up with more popular activities again. This is kind of like making a sandwich with the hard work put in the middle between two slices of more reinforcing activities.

Chaining *Chaining* involves taking two or more relatively simple behaviors and combining them like links into a more complex chain of behaviors. For example, Dick might be taught to brush his teeth by first wetting his tooth brush, next putting paste on the brush, then moving the brush over his teeth. Or to first put on a shoe, then pull the laces tight, and finally tie the knot. The various steps are taught one after the other. Since we still want Dick to perform each step, chaining is not the same as shaping.

Backward chaining, reverse chaining There is also *backward chaining* or *reverse chaining* in which we start with the final link and build additional steps in front of each newly acquired behavioral step. For example, Jane might first be taught to move the brush over her teeth. (But we've already put the paste on for her.) Next she is taught to put tooth paste on the tooth brush herself. Now we have the short chain of putting on paste and brushing. Later we add taking out the tooth brush and so on to lengthen the chain thereby helping Jane to become more independent. Since the older links have been learned and practiced longer, they have received more reinforcement and become more firmly established than the newer links which are more distant from the goal behavior.

A stimulus that is paired with or that directly precedes reinforcement tends to acquire reinforcing qualities and often then works as a reinforcer itself. So each link in a chain has two functions or jobs, one in relation to the behavior before it and one in relation to the behavior behind it. It's kind of like the two relationships of being the child of your parents, but also being a parent of your child. Each link reinforces the behavior it follows and serves as an S^D to the behavior it precedes.

Each link becomes a reinforcer for the behavior that precedes it and an S^D that signals that more reinforcement is coming if the chain is continued. As the sequence or chain of behaviors leading to the goal begins and then continues, the chain builds up momentum and becomes more difficult to stop. Many of us have experienced this momentum when attempting to diet. If we have a cache of cookies squirreled away in a secret place, once we start the chain it gets harder and harder to stop, like a snowball rolling down hill, as we go through the chain of behaviors leading up to the eating of the cookie. Going to the room where the cookies are hidden, opening the cabinet, taking down the container, taking off the lid, and…well, you know the rest.

This happens with many consummatory behavior problems, not just eating cookies. (Think about smoking and drinking.) These behavioral habits are a lot easier to stop earlier in the chain. It may work even better to avoid the S^D (or temptation, or "near occasion of sin") to begin with. How many of us, how often, can really have just one bite if we let the chain go to the end? A potato chip company used to market their product with the slogan "Bet you can't eat just one!" And if we do, how many *one bites* do we have? And how often? This is a natural chain that we're better off breaking early.

Backward chaining is often an effective technique for memorizing lists, poems, prayers, songs, and the like. By working backwards, once we begin to recall and recite the piece, each successive section that comes along has been more firmly learned than the earlier sections, making it less likely that they will be forgotten and more likely that this piece will be successfully remembered and completed. Backward chaining often works faster than forward chaining, since the final link is closer to the reinforcer and the newly added links are both reinforced sooner and become effective reinforcers themselves sooner.

Many of these procedures are used together in combination to teach a new behavior. Behaviors are often acquired through shaping, strengthened through reinforcement, occasioned by S^{D}s, and combined into chains.

Although we've talked about chaining as a way to build new behaviors, chaining has also been used at times to weaken unwanted behaviors. By adding more and more steps to a process, the reinforcement is delayed more and more and made so remote that it loses its effectiveness. Sometimes grievance and consumer complaint processes are designed to be so lengthy and complicated that they discourage people from using them, or if they start, most people give up before following through to the end.

Fading Once a behavior is established through the use of reinforcers and discriminative stimuli such as direct artificial prompts or cues, these S^{D}s can be faded, or gradually removed from the situation, leaving more naturally occurring S^{D}s to prompt the behavior. Handwriting programs that use visual guides for the learner to first trace whole words or letters, then switch to partial letters with less and less of the letters provided to be traced, and finally just lined paper, while the quality of the student's writing continues to meet acceptable standards, are examples of the use of *fading*. We continue to reinforce the target behavior while slowly and progressively diminishing the S^D. Since the last links in a behavioral chain are generally the strongest, it is generally best to fade prompts from the end of the chain first.

Another example would be teaching Jane to cross a street safely. You first walk with Jane to the crosswalk. Then you might say, "OK, Jane, now stop and wait," and next you give a long list of detailed verbal prompts, such as "Look both ways," "Look at the pedestrian crossing lights to be sure they are green and say 'Walk!', rather than red and 'Don't Walk!'", and so on. When, with detailed prompts, Jane follows the correct sequence, the prompts are gradually faded to shorter, less specific prompts, as Jane continues to perform the same behavior, perhaps even a question such as "OK, we're at the corner, what do you do now?"

Have you ever taught a dog to come when called? You might have done it something like this: your verbal command "Come" was followed by pulling on the leash or rope, like reeling in a fish, then a more gentle tug as a reminder to get Lassie started, and eventually the verbal command "Come" alone was sufficient. You gradually *faded out* your assistance, until finally good old Lassie was coming all by herself when you called (assuming you treated Lassie nicely when she got to you, of course).

Generalization   *Generalization* has to do with the spread of the effects of stimuli and behaviors from specific instances to broader or more general situations. Technically there are different types of generalization but for us the most important has to do with getting Dick to appropriately use certain behaviors in a variety of situations. Sometimes after a lot of hard work in a unique highly structured situation a teacher might teach Dick to respond when she says "Good morning, Dick" by making good eye contact with her, smiling and saying "Good morning, Ms. Smith." But that's it. A more long-term goal of course would be for Dick to respond the same way to Mrs. Brown, the principal, and Mr. Jones, the custodian. If Jane has learned that Mrs. Robinson is a lady and says that Mrs. Robinson is a lady when she sees Mrs. Robinson, Jane might generalize this response by saying "lady" when she sees Ms. Smith, Mrs. Sullivan and Mrs. Ryan too. There are now more stimuli that lead to the same response, saying "lady." This is stimulus generalization.

Although, for many of us, once we've acquired or learned new behaviors it is easy for us to perform them any place, any time, for many special needs children and adults it is much more difficult. A lot of additional work may have to be put into helping the new behaviors to generalize to a wider variety of situations and eventually, it is hoped, to the good old natural environment. Sometimes we have to directly teach the new behavior in several different situations. Many of the methods used to assist with this generalization emphasize the use of stimulus control techniques. The process of getting the behavior to happen in a greater variety of settings and situations is sometimes called *transfer training*.

There is also response generalization, which describes what happens when the same stimulus leads to different responses. Jane may have learned to say "Mama" when she sees her mother. As time goes by she might start saying things like "Mommie," "Mother," or "Mom." This is response generalization since although the stimulus may have remained the same, there are now a greater number of responses to that stimulus.

Dick's speech therapist, Mrs. Sullivan, might find that she has taught Dick to speak very clearly when he is talking with her in the speech office. But Dick's classroom teacher says that when Dick gets back to class he falls back into his old bad habit of mumbling his words. So Mrs. Sullivan starts spending some time in the classroom with Dick. This enables her to see for herself just what happens when Dick is speaking. It puts her in a position to prompt Dick to speak clearly and either to reinforce his behavior when he does speak clearly or to correct him when he does not. Perhaps Mrs. Sullivan's presence will serve as an S^D for Dick to speak clearly in the classroom setting. Dick may find that his classmates pay more attention to him when his speech is easier for them to understand. Over time Dick gradually learns the habit of speaking clearly in the classroom, and other character-istics of the classroom begin to become S^Ds for clear speaking. So eventually Mrs. Sullivan can slowly fade herself out of the classroom while Dick's clear speaking behavior is maintained by natural consequences in the natural environment.

Attention When we talk about paying *attention* to something or someone, we're usually talking about a behavior of ours that recognizes or acknowledges the exis-tence of something or somebody. In human interactions our attention indicates that we notice that someone else is there. Since people are social beings, one of the most powerful reinforcers to most of us is attention from other people. If we think about it, whenever we receive almost any reinforcement from anybody, we are also getting attention from them. As a result, attention can pick up a lot of rein-forcing qualities from its association with other reinforcers. The more important the person giving the attention is to the person getting the attention, the more powerful as a reinforcer that attention usually is. Attention can come in many forms: a smile, a word, a physical touch, a meeting of eyes, a laugh, a punch, a kick. These are all forms of attention. So attention can usually be used to increase a behavior and, as we said earlier, this would be considered positive reinforcement.

In a classroom, attention can come from anyone. Both teacher and peer atten-tion can be very powerful reinforcers. The attention doesn't have to be what could generally be thought of as nice or pleasant attention in order for it to be reinforc-ing. In classroom situations, teacher reprimands sometimes reinforce the unwanted behavior, or at best are neutral and ineffective. Sometimes getting yelled at by a teacher in front of a class can be very reinforcing. The public nature of a teacher's reprimand in front of a classroom full of giggling peers can really compli-cate the situation. Instead of decreasing the behavior the teacher wishes to reduce, it may actually serve to increase it. *Soft reprimands* is a term used to describe talking quietly to Dick in a public situation so that the reprimand is not heard by classmates and is less likely to reinforce the unwanted behavior. The same reprimand given more publicly may serve as a reinforcer.

As we discussed earlier, by withholding attention right after a behavior you want to decrease, you may be extinguishing it. The behavior would not extinguish, of course, if the attention withheld was not reinforcing the behavior in the first place. People will often try ignoring a behavior they hope will go away, but it may not seem to do any good. Well, if that's the case, it probably is something else, possibly attention from someone else, which is reinforcing the behavior in the first place. And of course attention from some people in some situations can be very aversive and function as a punisher, particularly for young children, or for an ado-lescent being teased or harassed by peers.

One very common way of giving attention to someone is by giving them a compliment. When trying to give verbal compliments we want to make sure that the words we choose really do work as reinforcing compliments. Usually if the child just understands what the words mean ("You drew that picture of a tree beautifully, Jane!"), that gets the job done. At other times the words might not seem to have formal dictionary definitions that literally make it clear that they are intended as compliments, but the context in which they are used and the enthusiasm with which they are given gets the message across. Forty-something years after I first saw the movie *Mary Poppins*, I still can't find supercalifragilisticexpialidocious in my dictionary, but I still know that if someone tells me that something I did was supercalifragilisticexpialidocious, it is probably meant as a compliment. When working with children who have more limited verbal repertoires and who have difficulty with the less-literal meaning of words, we need to be particularly sensitive to the effects of new verbal compliments that we may be using. Delivering these verbal compliments enthusiastically and occasionally pairing them with already established reinforcers can be a big help.

While using attention in the form of verbal compliments to reinforce good behavior when it occurs is usually a good idea, one problem that can come up is that repetitive and unenthusiastic-sounding compliments can soon begin to wear thin. Jane may only be able to hear "Very good, Jane!" so many times before she closes her ears and stops hearing it.

Fortunately, there are seemingly countless ways to give someone a compliment. In thinking about reinforcers we should keep in mind that variety is the spice of life and that nearly all reinforcers should be changed, or at least given a rest, from time to time. But we should balance this guideline with our awareness that some children really do *not* like change and variety. We need to be observant of what, if any, effects the changes we make in Dick's environment have on his behavior. The bottom line is: if it works like a reinforcer, it is a reinforcer. If it's not working like a reinforcer, it is not a reinforcer.

I have a cousin who is an elementary school teacher. She told me that when she started teaching some years ago her mother (my aunt) made her a wonderful list of things to say to compliment her students. There is a nice list of compliments that's been around for a while and that I've recently seen on several websites (e.g. www.careerlab.com/99ways.htm) entitled *99 Ways to Say Very Good*. This list was compiled by Arzella Dirksen, founder of *HelpCenter 4*, a television consumer hotline at KCNC television in Denver, Colorado, and is a good place to start to get some variety into what we are saying. Some other examples of variations that I've heard over the years include:

"Well done!"

"Nice!"

"I'm impressed!"

"All right!"

"You rock!"

"You're on a roll!"

"Way to go!"

"Bull's eye!"

"A 1!"

"Dyn-o-mite!"

"X O!" (I'm told that X O stands for kisses and hugs), and of course, "Supercalifragilisticexpialidocious!"

When attempting to give verbal reinforcement, it's important that Dick and Jane know just what it is that they did that we are complimenting. Just because we know what we're talking about doesn't mean that everyone else does too, particularly children. We shouldn't always take it for granted. So be ready to add specifics to your comments when there might be confusion, such as "Great job *on your spelling today Jane*" to help make sure you're on the same wavelength.

I'll bet you could add a lot more versions of "Very good!" to these lists too. But, most importantly, no matter how you say "Very good!," say it sincerely.

Differential reinforcement With some behaviors that we are trying to encourage we might be happy and willing to reinforce them any time, any place. This is particularly true when new desired behaviors are just being learned. But most behaviors are more appropriate in some situations than in other situations. *Differential reinforcement* refers to reinforcing a behavior in some situations, but not in other situations. These different situations could be the presence or absence of a particular stimulus. (Remember S^{D}s and S-deltas?) Jane's singing might be reinforced at choir practice but if she starts singing the same song during reading class, no reinforcement. Even though Jane's singing may be reinforced when she sings well at choir practice, Jane's singing may not be reinforced if she sings off key or if she sings too quickly.

Strategies for the classroom

Remember back in Chapter 4 we talked about continuous, intermittent, and ratio reinforcement schedules? Well, the scheduling of reinforcement doesn't stop there.

DRO   One type of differential reinforcement that is commonly used to weaken and eliminate troublesome behaviors is called *differential reinforcement of other behavior* (*DRO* for short, pronounced by just saying the letters D, R, O). DRO is an application of interval reinforcement schedules. In *DRO* Jane is reinforced according to a set schedule as long as she does not perform the target behavior during that time period. In DRO any other behavior except the target behavior is reinforced. While DRO can lead to rapid reduction of the target behavior, there is the danger of accidentally strengthening another undesirable behavior. Although extinction and time out (later in this chapter) are typically not very effective in treating behaviors maintained by automatic reinforcement, DRO and other types of differential reinforcement can be helpful.

DRI   A second kind of differential reinforcement is *DRI*, or *differential reinforcement of incompatible behavior*. In DRI Dick must be performing a behavior that is incompatible with the target behavior, a behavior that can not be performed at the same time. For example, if Dick chews his fingernails, he may receive scheduled reinforcement if he is clapping his hands, playing a musical instrument, or swinging a baseball bat, none of which could be done with his fingers in his mouth. So in DRI there are two conditions: the target behavior is not occurring and another behavior is being performed that makes it impossible to perform the target behavior at the same time. Substituting effective, useful adaptive behaviors for unwanted maladaptive behaviors with which they are incompatible is a common practice in ABA and behavior therapy.

DRA   *DRA* stands for *differential reinforcement of alternative behavior*. A lot of different things have been called DRA. At its broadest, a specific alternative behavior rather than just anything else but the target behavior (as in DRO) is selected for reinforcement. In the broad sense DRA is a lot like DRI except that the alternative behavior reinforced doesn't have to be incompatible with the target behavior. For example, Dick likes to amuse his friends and get his teacher's attention by poking Jane with his finger as they line up to go to art class. His teacher does not feel that she can try to extinguish this behavior by ignoring it. So she asks him to engage in an alternative behavior of checking off the names of each child on a class list. This is much more reinforcing to him, and he happily switches his behavior from poking to checking.

Remember one of the problems with using extinction was that we could end up with an extinction burst? Well, there are times, particularly when we are dealing with behaviors that are dangerous to the child or to others, that we just can't risk increasing the target behavior. Applications of DRA have sometimes been effective in getting rid of the maladaptive behavior without getting that nasty old extinction burst. In using DRA for this purpose we first must figure out what the reinforcers are that are maintaining or keeping the maladaptive target behavior going. Then, instead of just stopping the reinforcement, we select another alternative behavior and provide the same reinforcement for that behavior. Did I say the same reinforcement? While we do use the same reinforcers, we pay them out on a more dense or richer reinforcement schedule.

For example, one day, when especially frustrated, Jane started crying and scratching her arms severely in class. When she did this Ms. Thurber, the teacher's assistant, took Jane aside and talked to her to calm her down. Jane really enjoyed this individual attention from Ms. Thurber and started to cry and scratch more often, as often as once every day, with Ms. Thurber continuing to calm her down. If we were to try to eliminate Jane's bad habit by having Ms. Thurber ignore Jane when she acts up, chances are good that Jane would cry and scratch herself even more intensely in hopes of having Ms. Thurber give her attention again. This would be very disruptive to the class as well as seriously harmful to Jane. So we give Jane an alternative way to get some time alone with Ms. Thurber. We might arrange things so that whenever Jane successfully completes a class activity she and Ms. Thurber take a five-minute walk around the school together, which could happen several times each day.

We now have two alternative behaviors being reinforced with the same reinforcer, Ms. Thurber's attention, but on different reinforcement schedules. There is no longer any need for Jane to resort to hurting herself to get Ms. Thurber's attention. By adding additional reinforcement to Jane's life we have also increased her general level of reinforcement, which is usually a good idea when attempting to eliminate a previously reinforced behavior. When all this is done and the maladaptive target behavior is a thing of the past, we can gradually thin the reinforcement schedule for the alternative behavior to a lower level while maintaining the same rate of behavior and avoiding that extinction burst (we hope).

Limited hold One schedule that just about every parent and teacher has used is called *limited hold*. Limited hold is pretty much just what it sounds like. The payoff is available for a limited time only. A coupon from a restaurant for $22 off the cost of a meal would be an example of something I just lost out on by missing the expiration date while I was writing this book. Or: "Dick, if you put your toys away before I count to ten I'll read you a story." Another example would be if Jane has to turn in a book report by Friday in order to receive credit for the report.

DRH   *DRH*, or *differential reinforcement of high rates of behavior*, is a way to speed up slow pokes. Generally the target behavior must be repeated several times within a relatively short time period to receive reinforcement. Not too long ago I heard a story on the news about some skinny little guy who won a prize for eating the most hot dogs in something like 15 minutes. DRH. Jane may need to complete ten math problems in one minute to get an A, if it takes her two minutes she gets a B, or three minutes a C. Jane's teacher may offer a prize to all the students who can write the names of ten presidents in one minute.

DRL   *DRL*, on the other hand, stands for *differential reinforcement of low rates of behavior* (as if you didn't guess that yourself by now) and can be used to slow things down. A speech therapist working with a student who talks too rapidly might use DRL to help the student learn to slow down and speak more clearly at a more understandable rate. Teachers often have to work hard to encourage students to participate in class. Sometimes, though, a student becomes an overenthusiastic participant and starts monopolizing things by asking question after question after question. The teacher doesn't want to eliminate Dick's participation entirely, just reduce it to a more reasonable level so other students have a chance too. So the teacher decides to reinforce Dick's attempts to participate by only calling on him when he's gone at least two minutes without trying to ask a question.

Contingency contract, behavioral contract   A *contingency contract* is sometimes called a *behavioral contract*. It is easier to change behavior if the persons whose behaviors are being changed know exactly what they are supposed to do and what the consequences will be both if they perform acceptably and if they do not. Although it is not always necessary, it is often helpful to write this down in a formal contingency contract. A contingency contract is simply a written (usually) statement of what the student is expected to do and what the consequences will be. You might have a contract at work that, among other things, says that for every hour you work you will be paid X dollars. The contract normally follows the form "If you do A, then I will do B" or "If you do A, then you can do B."

   Once the contract is written up, it can be helpful to make additional copies and have a formal signing by all parties involved and a witness or two. The formality of some sort of ceremony can help to motivate children to comply with the conditions of a contract. It is also helpful for them to have a written reminder of just what is expected of them. The social presence of family, thereby involving important adults in the child's life, can help the contract get off to a good start.

Sometimes contracts that seem like good ideas at the time have unforeseen loopholes or other problems built in. It is a good idea to read the proposed contract from the child's point of view to try to spot potentially awkward problems. Initially the contract should be written for a limited time period, no longer than one week, to allow the adults to gracefully get out of it and renegotiate if there is an unseen loophole or some other problem.

Token economy   Another useful technique in a classroom situation is some form of a *token economy*. We already know that the reinforcement, or punishment, or response cost, or whatever we choose to use, should follow immediately after the target behavior or else we risk modifying the wrong behavior. While it is not always practical to distribute reinforcers immediately, it is nearly always possible to administer generalized secondary reinforcers such as tokens, chips, stars, points, stickers or tickets as substitutes that can later be redeemed or exchanged for backup reinforcers. This is especially helpful with children who are insufficiently motivated by rewards or other incentives that to them seem so far in the future that they lose their reality and therefore their effectiveness. Giving them something tangible brings the future reward much closer in terms of effectiveness. This is the principle that the famous S & H Green Stamps of years past worked on. The behavior the stores wanted to increase was the customers' spending their money. So as soon as customers paid for whatever they bought, the customers were immediately given some green stamps that they could save up and eventually redeem for a choice of reinforcers.

Reinforcement menu   The S & H Green Stamps company published a catalog with a list of prizes or reinforcers the customer could choose from. The catalog also listed the price of the reinforcers in numbers of green stamps. This catalog was an example of what we call a *reinforcement menu*.

A reinforcement menu can be drawn up which is a list of reinforcers that the child can choose from. Each item should have a designated price. The price is the number of tokens the item costs. Reinforcement menus are usually constructed to go along with token programs. This helps reduce the chance of *reinforcer satiation*. If only one reinforcer is used pretty soon most anyone will get tired of it and it will lose its effectiveness. But by providing a selection of reinforcers to choose from, we increase the probability that we have something that is appealing. It is also helpful to use reinforcers that can only be obtained by performing the behaviors required by the program and that are not readily available in another way. Additionally, the menu items available should be changed periodically, and the students involved should have some say in choosing the new reinforcers, and be kept up to date regarding the changes.

Reinforcement area   Some teachers set up what we call *reinforcement areas* in their rooms. This might be a table with a selection of toys, books, games, puzzles, and other fun activities. The children can earn access to this area for varying lengths of time (e.g. five to ten minutes) by producing school work or other forms of desirable behavior. This technique also helps lessen the problem of reinforcer satiation.

Discrete trial training   *Discrete trial training* refers to certain structured intense teaching strategies that are sometimes used to teach very specific behaviors. These approaches can be highly scripted and repetitive involving a series of repetitive trials employing the same antecedent, behavior, and consequences. For example, a teacher might sit right across a small table from the student, and prompt the student to name certain letters that they are shown over and over again. This can be a useful way to teach certain things to certain students, but can be very intense, and if not carefully monitored, risks becoming an aversive experience for some students. Also, there is usually little generalization from this approach alone, so other procedures need to be used to help generalize the performance of the newly learned behavior from the highly artificial environment to the more natural environment.

Response cost   We talked a bit about *response cost* back in Chapter 4. To refresh your memory, response cost is an aversive procedure but without as many drawbacks as punishment. A fine is a type of response cost that can easily be built into contingency contracts. While a list of fines can be included in a written contract, either with or without a contract it can be helpful to publicly post a fine schedule. When using fine systems or any response cost based intervention it is important not to let the students get too far in debt.

   If you are using both reinforcement and response cost procedures at the same time, the reinforcers that can be earned should not be the same as those that can be lost. Once a reinforcer is earned it should almost always be delivered (but perhaps delayed), even if undesirable behavior is costing the individual other reinforcers.

Time out   *Time out* (short for time out from reinforcement) is a term we hear a lot these days, but the name *time out* and the procedure *time out* are both often misused.

Sometimes we either can not find out what is reinforcing a specific behavior or there are so many things reinforcing the behavior that it just isn't practical to control them all. If this is the case and we really want to control the behavior at hand, we must then remove Dick from the reinforcer-loaded immediate environment. We often accomplish this by placing Dick in a *time-out* area, which is usually a room or space without reinforcers. (Does solitary confinement ring a bell?)

Properly applied, time out should involve the separation of Dick from all sources of reinforcement, either by withdrawing reinforcement from the situation or by removing Dick from the situation that has reinforcers in it, perhaps by sending him to a corner, behind a partition, or to a nearby room. This should immediately follow the target behavior, but should be for a relatively brief length of time. Ten to fifteen minutes per episode is usually sufficient. A good rule of thumb to use is one minute in time out for each year of the child's age, so a seven-year-old might get seven minutes in time out. But going much beyond ten minutes, assuming there is no tantruming or other maladaptive behavior going on, may be counterproductive. When an episode of tantruming of some sort is occurring, the start of the timing of the time-out period is often delayed until the tantruming ends. In the complicated real world of learning in a natural environment, time out probably includes elements of punishment, response cost, and extinction. But in some cases time out can function as a positive reinforcer, or even a negative reinforcer if the child is over-stimulated in the natural environment. After all, don't we all enjoy a little peace and quiet once in a while?

The two most important things to remember about time out are that it must follow immediately after the target behavior so that there can be no opportunity for reinforcement from the environment and the time-out area must have nothing about it which is likely to be reinforcing. This includes no one to talk to, listen to, or to watch. Delaying the implementation of the consequences to explain in detail, negotiate, argue, bargain, plead, beg, barter, or whatever can significantly reduce or totally negate any effectiveness the intended consequence might have had.

Many of the things we do in ABA involve gradual changes of one sort or another. In shaping we reinforced a succession of behaviors that gradually became more and more like the target behavior. In thinning we gradually lessened the frequency of reinforcement used to maintain the behavior and in fading we gradually diminished the prompts we were using to encourage a behavior while keeping the behavior pretty much the same.

Demand fading   Another term that includes the word fading is *demand fading*. Demand fading usually involves the gradual tightening of the demands placed on the child in order to continue receiving reinforcement. Demand fading is mostly used with children who have a tendency to tantrum to escape or avoid the situation when certain demands are placed on them. Usually when we think of fading we think of something diminishing or getting smaller in one way or another, like the fading of a color in an over-washed shirt, but fading sometimes is used to describe gradually fading something in, or increasing it, like when the loudness of the sound track of a movie is gradually increased.

Dick might typically eat five bites of an apple. When he's told he now needs to eat ten bites, he is a good bet to throw a tantrum to get out of eating the apple. So when things are going pretty good we might fade-in one additional bite, going from a demand of five bites to a demand of six bites, until this increase is accepted. Then up to seven bites and so on. This kind of reminds me of price increases at the store or gas pump.

There are a number of procedures used to reduce certain kinds of inappropriate behaviors that seem to be good old-fashioned common-sense types of punishment.

Correction   The term *correction* means pretty much what it sounds like it means. If you make a mess you clean it up. Sometimes tantruming children knock things over and throw things around. Picking up and putting things back the way they were would be forms of correction.

Overcorrection   *Overcorrection* refers to correction and then some. Maybe Dick is caught writing graffiti on a wall. In addition to cleaning off the graffiti that he wrote on that wall, our friend may also be required to clean the other walls in that room.

Positive practice   *Positive practice* is a type of overcorrection in which the child essentially rehearses doing something properly over and over again. If Jane shouts "Give me a cookie!" she might be required to politely ask "May I please have a cookie?" five times before receiving the cookie.

Negative practice   *Negative practice* involves performing the target behavior over and over, without reinforcement, as a way of decreasing the maladaptive behavior. Negative practice has been used effectively to help in the treatment of behaviors such as tics, stuttering and other repetitive behavior patterns including bad habits that people sometimes engage in without realizing it, such as repetitive knuckle-cracking.

Negative practice has a lot of potential for misuse. If Dick performed an inappropriate behavior such as swearing, and was required to repeat that same behavior over and over again until the act of swearing became aversive to him, it would be considered negative practice. But with Dick and in nearly all cases there are better ways to deal with the target behaviors. Actually it's been quite a while since I've heard of it being used like this. I hope that you won't hear of it very often, if at all.

Since we're talking about types of practice, there are two other types of practice that I should mention which are used to strengthen learning.

Massed practice   *Massed practice* refers to a situation in which the same behavior is repeated over and over in a relatively short time period. In some ways massed practice is like an extreme form of positive practice. Cramming for an exam can be thought of as a type of massed practice that many of us have experienced at one time or another. If Jane has a spelling test on Friday, she might wait until Thursday night and study the same words over and over for an hour.

Distributed practice   *Distributed practice* is an approach to learning in which you don't put all your eggs in one basket, as you might with massed practice, but spread your practice out in smaller doses over a longer period of time. If Jane plans ahead for that spelling test and studies the same words for 15 minutes each night for the four nights Monday through Thursday, she still ends up studying the same words for the same total time of one hour. Assuming that enough studying or practice actually happens to learn whatever it is you're trying to learn, distributed practice usually results in better long-term memory or recall of whatever it is that we learned. When you just crammed for an exam you might have done well on the test the next day, but how long did you really remember after that?

Social Skills

Social Skills Training   *Social skills training* is a term that describes any of several approaches used to teach people how to appropriately interact with other people. Targeted behaviors in social skills training often include behaviors such as eye contact, keeping appropriate social distance, and hand shaking. Video equipment can be a very helpful tool in both modeling appropriate behavior and providing feedback to students.

Much of the early research on social skills training dealt with teaching "dating" skills to college students. This was for several reasons, not the least of which was the ease in getting students to volunteer to be subjects for the research. A great deal of psychological research is conducted by faculty and graduate students at universities because that is where they (the researchers) already are and they have a large pool of potential subjects (undergraduate students) to draw from. The student volunteers are often given small payments or extra credit in psychology courses for their help. Add to this that most college students want to improve their social lives anyway. Bingo! All the volunteers you'd ever need.

Back in Chapter 5 we talked about the difference between acquisition problems and performance problems. Making this distinction is particularly important during social skills training. Many people have already learned or acquired the appropriate social repertoire for a given social situation, but may be inhibited from using their social behavior effectively by emotional factors such as social anxiety. This is primarily a performance problem. For these people the treatment emphasis is likely to be on their emotional behaviors, perhaps by using forms of desensitization or assertiveness training. For other people they might feel perfectly comfortable in social situations but just don't know the right thing to do or how to do it. For them it's an acquisition problem first, then perhaps a performance problem. Jane might very nicely demonstrate an appropriate way of introducing herself to a new classmate when role playing, but may be prevented by anxiety when in real-life situations (performance problem). Dick may feel reasonably at ease, but might not know what to say to his new classmate (acquisition problem).

Although social skills can be taught in several different ways, many social skills training programs include the four steps of Structured Learning Therapy (Goldstein, Sprafkin and Gershaw 1976): *modeling, role playing, social reinforcement,* and *transfer training*. Suppose there is a problem with Dick's just reaching out and grabbing other children's snacks whenever he wants to. Our goal might be to have Dick ask nicely, saying something like "Jane, may I please have one of your cookies?" We might first demonstrate to Dick by saying ourselves, "Jane, may I please have one of your cookies?" Next we role play that we are perhaps Jane and have Dick say to us, "Jane, may I please have one of your cookies?" In the role-play situation we give Dick *social reinforcement* for performing socially appropriate behavior (sometimes called *prosocial behavior*) by praising him and occasionally actually giving him a cookie.

Video modeling Teaching social skills to children by having them watch videos of others demonstrating various social behaviors has been found to work well with many ASD children. *Video modeling,* as this procedure is called, has been particularly effective in teaching play skills. If you want to learn more about using video modeling you'll probably find the book *Video Modeling and Behavior Analysis* (Nikopoulos and Keenan 2006) helpful.

Social Stories™   A well-known method for teaching social skills to individuals with ASDs that can also be helpful with most younger children is the *Social Stories* ™ approach developed by Carol Gray (Gray and White 2002). Social Stories ™ are an application of modeling that involve very brief, often illustrated, stories that model for the child the step-by-step performance of various social skills, basic self-help safety, and hygiene behaviors.

Behavioral rehearsal   Combining role play of appropriate social behavior with the desired consequences is sometimes referred to as *behavioral rehearsal*. A series of scenarios, including the hoped-for consequences, can be practiced. As the child becomes more skillful in performing these behaviors the therapist may add surprise complications to the situation to help the child learn to behave appropriately in a greater variety of situations. Once Dick has acquired the new social behavior and can adequately demonstrate the behavior in the artificial staged rehearsal situation, it is important that we help transfer the new behavior to real-life social situations where he will be able to use it effectively.

Transfer training   Transfer training is a term sometimes used to describe the general process of helping Jane to perform certain behaviors in new situations. This can be thought of as a kind of stimulus generalization. Depending on the situation, many additional steps may need to be added between some of these steps. We want to have manageable steps as we move from inappropriate social behavior toward more appropriate social behavior. Transfer training and generalization are both important to the spreading of new behaviors from carefully controlled prosthetic and therapeutic environments to more natural environments as the student is taken out to learn to deal with the real world.

Guided practice   In some cases verbal instructions and modeling aren't very effective in getting the message across about just what it is that we want Jane to do and how we want her to do it. This is particularly true when we're talking about motor behaviors. Sometimes physical guidance of the proper movements is helpful; this is termed *guided practice*. If Jane's parents are trying to teach her to hit a thrown softball with a bat, maybe her mother will stand right behind Jane with her hands on Jane's hands and guide her through a swing as Dad pitches the ball.

Relaxation training   Being able to relax is important for all of us. It helps us concentrate better when we are trying to pay attention to something and helps us settle down when we are angry, fearful, or otherwise emotionally upset, and being relaxed can help lessen the experience of pain. Various forms of *relaxation training* have been taught for years in all sorts of areas such as stress management training, child birth classes, sport psychology, and the treatment of anxiety disorders. While there are numerous ways to learn to relax, perhaps the best known of the behavioral approaches is *progressive muscle relaxation* or PMR. Through progressive muscle relaxation we are taught to tense and then relax various muscle groups throughout our bodies, first individually and eventually all at once. This is a very useful self-control device that absolutely everyone has need for at some time or other.

People can be taught to use this technique to calm themselves down when they are upset or in anticipation of stressful situations before they occur. *Relaxation: A Comprehensive Manual for Adults, Children and Children with Special Needs* (Cautela and Groden 1978) is a very helpful guide book that describes how to individualize PMR for children with special needs. In teaching PMR it is often helpful to have the students learning the technique take the lead in directing group relaxation sessions for classmates. By talking their way through the process aloud and demonstrating to the group, they tend to learn the procedure better themselves and gain more confidence in its use.

Well, there are countless more ways that ABA can be used that we could talk about, including ways ABA can be used for primarily educational purposes. That's where we'll pick it up in Chapter 8.

Chapter 8

WHAT IS BEHAVIORAL EDUCATION?

As we talked about earlier, ABA has very wide applicability. Not all applications deal with maladaptive behavior. There are many applications that we see mostly in schools that are very useful in general education as well as special education.

Behavioral education   The use of programs and procedures based on behavioral principles in schools and other educational settings is sometimes called *behavioral education*.

Direct instruction   One of the best-known contributions to education is *direct instruction*. Direct instruction involves a lot of scripted and sequenced instructions and prompts and requires the student to actively respond or perform a behavior correctly to receive positive reinforcement. The carefully prepared lessons have been tested and demonstrated to be effective with other students. Immediate correction of errors is an important ingredient. The lessons are presented at a fast pace. They are usually designed to have the students make at least ten active responses per minute. This high rate of student performance provides immediate feedback to the teacher so that any learning problems can be spotted and addressed as soon as possible.

DISTAR   Probably the best-known example of direct instruction is *DISTAR* (*Direct Instruction for the Teaching of Arithmetic and Reading*) developed by Siegfried Engelmann and his colleagues. For some reason they keep changing the name of the DISTAR programs. I think it's also been called *Reading Mastery* and is related to other programs such as *Horizon* and *Funnix*. While DISTAR reading is the best known, there are DISTAR programs for math and language as well as reading.

Errorless learning   People tend to find learning more pleasant and learn more when they have a high success rate. Wouldn't you rather get a 95 percent on a test than a 5 percent? Plus remember that whenever we do something we are practicing it and even though the old saying goes "practice makes perfect," a more accurate saying is "practice makes permanent." If we practice something over and over, whether right or wrong, it becomes a more firmly established habit, so better to be practicing doing something right than practicing doing it wrong. Much of behavioral education requires a lot of activity or behaving on the part of the students, demonstrating what they are learning as they go along. *Errorless learning* has to do with arranging things in a learning program to maximize success, like shaping, going from the known to the closely related unknown. When a mistake is made, usually additional prompts are given until the right response (which could be a verbal answer or some other action) is emitted, then immediate reinforcement and on we go…

Precision teaching   Although *precision teaching* is a thoroughly behavioral approach to education it has a vocabulary of its own. One of Skinner's graduate students, Ogden Lindsley, is sometimes called the father of precision teaching. Now I wrote this book in the first place to help translate some of the specialized vocabulary of ABA into what I hope is plain English. Wouldn't you know it, even though precision teaching is a specialized application of ABA, Lindsley (Og, as he was known to his friends) thought the ABA vocabulary was too "jargony" and tried to come up with more easily understood alternatives for a lot of other ABA words. For example, in the precision teaching world the term *movement* is used rather than behavior. Remember Og's Dead Man Rule? Dead men shouldn't be moving, so they don't behave. Increasing or strengthening a behavior is referred to as *accelerating* while weakening or decreasing the rate of a behavior is called *decelerating*. *Pinpointing* is identifying the behavior or movement to be targeted and counted. *Aims* refers to the target rate at which, it is hoped, the behavior will be performed. There are no mistakes or failures in precision teaching, just correct responses and *learning opportunities*.

Three of the most important components of precision teaching are daily measurements of correct and incorrect responses, using standard charts to record and display these daily behavioral rates, and using this objective data to make data-based decisions about how best to teach the students. Actually, precision teaching is less of a teaching method and more of a means to evaluate the effectiveness of methods used in teaching. Skinner's daughter, Dr. Julie Vargas, who is a professor of behaviorology in the Department of Educational Psychology and Foundations at West Virginia University, has suggested that *precision measurement* might be a better term to use since the emphasis is on the accurate measurement of the effects of teaching rather than a specific teaching method. To paraphrase Skinner again, "if there isn't learning, there wasn't any teaching."

Fluency One of the key concepts of precision teaching is *fluency*, which is a combination of accuracy and speed. We see the importance of fluency in many areas, such as reading, athletics, music, and speaking. When I was in high school I could do a pretty good job of accurately translating French into English and vice versa, but it took me a long time and I needed to use a French/English dictionary as well as a French text book with French grammar. I could eventually get the job done and even pronounce many of the words fairly accurately, but I certainly couldn't be considered fluent in French. The same idea can be applied to other areas such as reading, writing, and arithmetic. People who are fluent commit few errors and perform competently at an effective rate for whatever it is they are doing. Fluency can be thought of as mastery of the subject matter. Some call it *automaticity*.

Precision teachers have *improved fluency* as one of their major goals and use many timing techniques to measure and record improvements in fluency. One-minute timings are commonly used to assess improved learning of, for example, addition of two-digit numbers. Jane may be given work sheets with numerous two-digit addition problems of similar difficulty. Then she is timed to see how many of the problems she can correctly answer in one minute.

Fluency is an important element that is often overlooked in educational plans. Three benefits of achieving fluency are longer retention of what was learned, increased endurance or stamina in performing the behavior, and increased ease in transferring the new skills to new situations.

Standard celeration chart, standard behavior chart The results of these precision teaching timings are recorded on specialized graph paper called *standard celeration charts* or *standard behavior charts*. These charts are printed with lots of blue lines and look pretty confusing at first, but really aren't that bad.

Charting *Charting* is what precision teachers call keeping track of the data on standard celeration charts. The precision teaching motto is "Care enough to chart."

SAFMEDS Another precision teaching term you may hear is *SAFMEDS*. What the heck is a SAFMED, you ask? Well, SAFMEDS is an acronym, one of those words made up of the first letter of a bunch of other words for easy remembering. In this case SAFMEDS stands for "Say All Fast, Minute Each Day, Shuffled." What this basically amounts to is a teaching technique based on using flash cards to help Jane learn something, maybe the state capitals, by presenting them to her every day for a one-minute timing, but shuffling them each time so that she doesn't just memorize a sequence list.

Although this precision teaching stuff may sound pretty complicated, once the children get used to it they often have the responsibility of recording their own behaviors. There is a classic instructional slide-tape presentation from around 1970 called *Charting Rates with Stephanie Bates*, which has a kindergarten student, Stephanie Bates, explaining and demonstrating how to use the standard celeration chart for charting behavior.

Programmed instruction   *Programmed instruction* is a term used to describe employing principles of learning to choose and organize the content of what is being taught (curriculum) and how it is to be taught. There are all sorts of variations to programmed instruction, but it is more commonly thought of as being used at the college level for introductory and other psychology and education courses.

PSI   *PSI* is not the name of a hit TV show but stands for *personalized system of instruction*. PSI was developed by Skinner's good buddy and fellow graduate student at Harvard, Fred Keller. PSI is an application of individualized instruction. It involves a progress-at-your-own-pace component and the requirement to demonstrate mastery at various points before advancing further through the curriculum. While mechanical teaching machines and programmed texts were often used in PSI, many of the programmed texts and the mechanical teaching machines have been largely replaced by computers. In PSI, quizzes are used to determine when the student has achieved sufficient mastery to move on to the next unit, rather than to come up with a grade.

Programmed text   A particularly interesting and often enjoyable form of programmed instruction that you might have already run into are *programmed texts*. Books written in programmed text format help readers to learn better what they have read. An excellent and well-known book that presents a behavioral approach to childhood problem behavior, *Living With Children* (Patterson 1976), is a good example of a book written in (1) _____ text format, to help readers learn what they are reading. Programmed texts are often written in a fill-in-the-blank format with prompted answers provided nearby for quick self-monitoring and self-correction, if needed. This approach makes it easier for readers to (2) _____ what they are reading about as they go along. Reading a programmed text might not always go as quickly as reading a more typical book. Programmed texts encourage active learning by prompting behavior as the reader is guided to behave actively and overtly along the way. The reader is (3) _____ to provide answers to various questions about what is being read. By the end of the book the reader hasn't just gotten to the end of the book passively. Instead at the end we have a reader who has actively acquired more of the knowledge of the book content, and, by overtly (4) _____ by completing the sentences with the correct answer, has strengthened that learning still further. When the material is particularly difficult and when writing for younger readers, stronger discriminative stimuli are often used to occasion the correct answer. An example of this might be something like "Events that occasion behavior are called (5) d __ __ c __ __ __ __ __ __ __ __ __ __ s __ __ __ __ __ __ __ ."*

Actually this section on programmed texts is written in programmed text format, and this wasn't too bad, was it?

Match to sample *Match to sample* is another behavioral teaching technique that is pretty much just what it sounds like. The child is shown a sample of something and a group of comparison choices to possibly match the sample. The child is directed to choose the best match for the sample, like multiple choice. In a simple example the correct match can be identical to the sample such as a green block or a yellow crayon. But in a more complex example, match to sample may be used to teach word recognition. The word "cat" might be shown on a card and Dick is shown pictures of several animals to choose from, including of course a cat. The correct choice results in immediate reinforcement.

*Answers:
1. programmed
2. learn
3. prompted
4. behaving
5. discriminative stimuli

Stimulus equivalence In more complex situations the matching stimuli are not identical, but are equivalent in what they represent. Did you ever hear in math class that if A = B and B = C, then A = C? It's sort of the same idea. Suppose the symbol 🐕 represents a picture of a dog that we see in a book, D O G represents the word written out using the letters D, O, G, and "dog" represents the sound of the spoken word dog. These three stimuli are all symbols that represent the concept of dog, and should all get the idea of dog across, so they are all considered equivalent stimuli. Interestingly, in most cases when two of these relations are directly taught, such as 🐕 (pictured) = D O G (written), and 🐕 = "dog" (spoken), the individual will usually make the connection D O G (written) = "dog" (spoken) on her own. So now if Jane hears the word "dog," she could select 🐕 or the written word D O G, and so on, even though she's never been taught this directly.

This is essentially what people mean when they talk about understanding something. *Stimulus equivalence* and its applications can get a lot more complicated, but that's beyond what we need to know for now. Teaching stimulus equivalence relationships is particularly helpful in language training. Although this is another topic for another place, you might be interested to know that stimulus equivalence can contribute to the spread of phobias and other emotional reactions as well.

If you're interested in learning more about what is happening in behavioral education these days, you might find the professional journals *Education and Treatment of Children*, published by The Roscoe Ledger, and *The Journal of Behavioral Education*, published by Springer Science and Business Media, interesting.

As I'm sure you know, the ability to communicate is critical to humans. ABA has proven to be very useful in helping people to learn to communicate more effectively. In the ABA world we refer to communication-related behaviors as verbal behavior.

Language and verbal behavior

We briefly talked about verbal behavior at the very end of Chapter 2. Here are a few more terms you might hear when talking about verbal behavior.

Functional communication training When people have trouble expressing their needs they can get pretty frustrated and act up in one way or another. Sometimes this acting up or misbehaving leads to reinforcement such as attention. This often happens with individuals with severe speech and language deficits. *Functional communication training* (FCT) refers to teaching alternate ways of communicating so that individuals with severe language deficits can express themselves more successfully. This enables them to get their reinforcement by having their needs met without resorting to maladaptive behaviors. In these communication systems, behaviors other than spoken language function or work as language since they enable the child to successfully communicate with others. Sign language and the Picture Exchange Communication System are two examples of FCT.

PECS   *PECS* stands for the *Picture Exchange Communication System*. PECS is a program designed to teach beginning communication skills to people with serious communication disorders. PECS involves several phases of training, starting with teaching the child to exchange a picture of a reinforcer for the actual reinforcer and leading up to communicating about things in the environment. Pictures are used to represent common objects, and symbols are often used for other common words. PECS enables children who can not yet communicate successfully through speech to express themselves successfully by using a series of pictures. Verbal prompting is not usually used during PECS lessons. PECS can be taught and used by parents.

ABLLS   *ABLLS* is short for the *Assessment of Basic Language and Learning Skills*. The ABLLS is a systematic behavioral assessment tool designed to help identify skill deficits in language and other important areas (e.g. several verbal behaviors, self-help skills, pre-academic skills) that children usually learn from daily experiences.

More ways to enhance learning

Spiral learning   *Spiral learning* is a circular spiral teaching approach. We keep coming back over several topics, going into greater or additional detail each time, sort of like desensitization, and involving distributed learning. Have you noticed parts of this book have been somewhat repetitive, going back to touch on topics introduced in earlier chapters, but often adding additional details the second time around?

Overlearning   *Overlearning* is another term we hear from time to time that isn't strictly an ABA term. Although this term has been used in different ways, overlearning generally refers to continuing to practice something even after the criteria for learning it has been met. Students who continue to review a list of the capitals of all of the countries belonging to the European Union, even after getting them all right in a practice test, a pianist who continues to practice a Mozart piece that she's been playing in concerts for years, an actor who continues to rehearse his lines for a play that's been running for weeks, a gymnast who continues to practice her medal-winning gymnastics routine are all engaging in overlearning. Someone who recites from memory a prayer first learned many years ago, in addition to receiving whatever benefits there may be for saying the prayer, is practicing overlearning.

A major hoped-for advantage of overlearning is that it can make the learned behavior more resistant to forgetting. Students who continue to study their math facts or spelling words may be able to still demonstrate this knowledge after long delays. Overlearning can also contribute to the likelihood of performing behaviors correctly in a particularly stressful situation such as taking a test or performing in front of an audience. Some people think of overlearning as a process that can lead to the fluency effect we talked about earlier.

Positive Behavior Support (PBS) *Positive Behavior Support* (PBS) is a movement that began as a reaction to what was seen as an overuse of aversive control measures with developmentally disabled individuals. PBS has an organization of its own, the Association for Positive Behavior Support (APBS) and holds conferences and conducts training to promote the use of PBS in schools and other settings. PBS employs many of the methods and procedures of ABA, and many PBS proponents are also behavior analysts.

CABAS *CABAS* is an acronym for *Comprehensive Application of Behavior Analysis to Schooling*. Doug Greer, of Columbia University's Teachers College, has developed a little something called CABAS which is a behaviorological systems approach that is more than just a reading program or token economy scattered here and there, but rather a system that thoroughly impacts the entire school from the ground up. Behavioral principles are applied to all members of the school community—students, teachers, supervisors and parents—to help them learn to perform their various roles more effectively. As of this writing there are CABAS demonstration schools for students up to grade six in the United States, Ireland, and England. The CABAS Board also offers certification for teachers and others who work in behavioral education.

In the last few chapters we've talked about some of the more common applications of behavioral principles that you are likely to encounter. There are others, of course, and depending on the particulars of the real-life circumstances and the creativity of those developing the behavioral programs, most of these procedures can be dressed up in a seemingly endless variety of ways to improve their effectiveness.

Chapter 9

SUMMING UP

Well, here we are, coming into the home stretch. Let's just take a few pages to go over some important guidelines to remember.

1. The reinforcement (or aversive consequence) should follow immediately after the behavior we want to modify. While it is not always practical to distribute reinforcers immediately, it is nearly always possible to administer substitutes such as tokens, stars, points or check marks which can be redeemed later for backup reinforcers. This is especially helpful with children who are not very motivated by rewards that to them seem so far in the future that they lose their reality and their effectiveness. Giving Dick and Jane something tangible brings the future reward much closer in terms of effectiveness.

2. Some of the most common reinforcers used in schools are specific classroom jobs, going to recess early, use of toys for a specified length of time, extra time in a resource room, and individual attention from teachers. Attention is one of the most powerful of all reinforcers. After all, attention is often an S^D that more reinforcement is coming. For some children any kind of attention at all is reinforcing, even the attention which comes with a scolding by a teacher or a beating from a parent. This is one of the reasons why reprimanding disruptive behavior sometimes has no effect on certain children. Actually, because of the attention involved, it may even be reinforcing the disruptive behavior.

3. Initially, small approximations of the desired behavior should be reinforced.

4. Reinforcement should be frequent, especially at first, but should be relatively small.

5. Reinforcers can be more effective if they are obtainable only as a consequence of performing the desired behavior.

6. Reinforcers should be varied. If Jane receives too much of one thing she soon becomes tired of it and it loses its reinforcing qualities. Reinforcement menus can help with this.

7. There is no such thing as a universal reinforcer. What is reinforcing (or aversive) to Dick is not necessarily reinforcing to Jane. We have to be very careful that what we choose to use as reinforcers really are reinforcers in the situation and for the person with whom they are to be used. No matter how nice we think something is, if it doesn't increase the behavior, in that situation at least, it is not a reinforcer.

8. It is important that Jane knows why she is being reinforced or punished. Presentation of a token should be accompanied by an explanation such as "You remembered to bring your homework today, Jane, so you earned this token."

9. The source of a reinforcement is important. A compliment from someone whose favor we are trying to win is usually more powerful than the same comment from someone we don't care about.

10. Reinforcement programs should be set up so that everyone involved can easily earn some reinforcers right from the start. If failure is met at the beginning, the children might be turned off by the program before it has a chance to work.

11. Any contract negotiated must be fair, honest, and clear.

12. Occasionally the problem arises of other children being envious of Dick if they feel he is receiving special treatment. This can be overcome by allowing Dick to earn reinforcers for the entire class. He is also likely to become more popular.

13. Sometimes it is possible to identify certain stimuli or conditions that seem to be causes or are always present when the target behavior occurs. Remember *discriminative stimuli*? If this is the case, then a change in these conditions is often enough to change the target behavior. For example, if Dick only acts up when he is sitting near a particular classmate the solution would seem to be to keep them separated in class.

The use of ABA principles and procedures in general has many advantages. Some of them are as follows:

1. ABA can be used with just about any kind of problem. Cautela and Ishaq (1996) published a book which includes many examples of the use of behavioral principals in a wide range of areas, including substance abuse, HIV (human immunodeficiency virus) prevention, college teaching, poverty, sport and exercise, and geriatrics.

2. ABA techniques are based on experimental evidence. If one technique doesn't work, it is discarded. Experimentation is encouraged, and there are all kinds of empirical evidence that behavior modification techniques are more effective than other approaches in treating similar kinds of problems.

3. ABA-based interventions can be more personal and less mechanistic than other approaches. Treatment procedures can be tailor made to fit individual students and their learning style and needs rather than treating every person in the same assembly-line manner, ignoring their individuality.

4. By setting objective, measurable, and observable behavioral goals, we can easily see if what we are doing is working.

5. Since everybody is modifying behavior all the time anyway, behavioral procedures can easily be applied in some form when working with children.

6. The results of behavior modification are often reversible. Whatever is learned can usually be unlearned and relearned.

You have probably recognized a lot of these principles and techniques as procedures that you already use or see used in working with children. As we talked about earlier, a great deal of behavior modification is really just a systematic and efficient use of common sense.

So now you are an informed consumer of ABA! Until you get more detailed training, however, let the professional experts do it. An introduction like this certainly can't be complete, but I hope that I've been able to explain much of the mysterious vocabulary and ideas used in the world of ABA. But if some of the explanations don't seem to make sense given what you see going on in your child's program, or if you hear other terms being used, by all means ask the "experts" who are using those terms to explain what they mean in plain English. Then you can add your own personalized appendix to the back of this book to make it more individualized and complete for your program. And if asking the experts isn't convenient, many of the books mentioned in the Appendix and listed in the References section have helpful explanations in the text and useful glossaries. Good luck, and remember to *catch them being good!*

Appendix

WHAT ELSE CAN
I READ ABOUT ABA?

If you would like any more information about behavior modification or possible help in applying these techniques with your children, here are some good books for more in-depth info on ABA. Most of these books do not require any specialized psychological training to understand, and are available in many schools' professional libraries. More complete information about the authors and publishers of these works can be found in the References section.

Two particularly good books for parents are *Living with Children*, by Gerald Patterson (1976), and *Parents are Teachers*, by Wesley Becker (1971). Many of the ABA principles you've been introduced to are discussed in greater depth, and ways of applying these principles to specific childhood behavior problems are suggested by the expert authors.

Social problems are a major issue that many children face, whether they are considered to have an ASD or not. A nice little book that deals with this issue and can be helpful to just about any adult reader is *Helping Kids Make Friends*, by Stocking, Arezzo and Leavitt (1979).

Steps to Independence (Baker *et al.* 2004) is a terrific resource for parents and other caregivers of special needs children. It includes programs for teaching a variety of everyday skills such as self-help, toileting, and play skills. The *Steps to Independence* series grew out of the authors' work at Camp Freedom, one of the first behaviorally oriented summer camps for children with special needs, back in the 1970s. Bruce Baker, the first author of *Steps to Independence*, was one of my first behavior modification teachers, so it's got to be old. But although it's been around for over 30 years, *Steps to Independence* has been through several updates and it's still in press, so you know it's got to be good!

Another good book for parents is *Changing Children's Behavior*, by the husband and wife team, John and Helen Krumboltz (1972). It lists many common childhood behavior problems and offers behaviorally based suggestions on how to deal with them.

There are also a growing number of newer books that are worth looking at. *Functional Behavior Assessment for People with Autism* by Beth Glasberg (2005) goes into greater detail about how to apply many of the concepts you've just read about. *Parents' Education as Autism Therapists*, edited by Keenan, Kerr and Dillenburger (1999), is an interesting collection of articles written by parents and professionals discussing various issues related to using ABA principles with autistic children. The authors are members of a group named Parents Education as Autism Therapists (or PEAT), established to help bring training in ABA to parents in Northern Ireland. It provides a good overview of ABA and many excellent case examples of parents using ABA treatment with their own children, under the supervision of ABA experts.

In addition there are a few excellent books written at the college text level that I'd like to mention. Murray Sidman's *Coercion and its Fallout* (1989) is a very thorough discussion of the pros and cons of the use of punishment and other aversive procedures. Sulzer and Mayer first published *Behavior Modification Procedures for School Personnel* back in 1972, but it is still a wonderful book that is a very thorough first text in ABA for people who may be working on the front lines with children in school settings.

Sidney Bijou's *Behavior Analysis of Child Development* (1995) is a short introductory book for students interested in child development from a behavioral point of view. It first appeared in 1961 with the most recent revision in 1995. Roland Tharpe and Ralph Wetzel's 1969 book *Behavior Modification in the Natural Environment* describes a successful consulting model they developed for delivering ABA treatment through the direct work of the "treaters" on the front lines, the parents, teachers, and other caretakers of behaviorally disordered children. This is a fairly advanced book, but might be of particular interest to behavior analysts and others involved with parent and teacher training and consultation programs.

Many of the behavioral programs used to help children include some form of token economy. Two books that you might find interesting if you are involved in setting up and managing a token economy are *The Token Economy* by Alan Kazdin (1977) and *The Token Economy* by Ted Ayllon and Nate Azrin (1968). (That's right. Both books have the same title. Seems confusing to me.) Kazdin's book is a great summary of historical background, types of token economies, and how to use and move beyond token economy systems. For the more historically interested reader Ayllon and Azrin write in detail about what is often considered to be the first token economy system, the program they developed at Anna State Hospital in Illinois, back in the 1960s.

Well now, if you have worked your way through *Understanding Applied Behavior Analysis* and perhaps a few of these other books, you may feel that you are ready for a scholarly text. If you do, a book I would recommend is Cooper, Heron and Heward's very thorough and well written text, simply titled *Applied Behavior Analysis*.

Actually, there are many books, CDs, DVD/videos and other materials available that can be very helpful for people living or working with children and adolescents. There are, however, certain publishing companies that seem to have a special interest in this area. In addition to Jessica Kingsley Publishers, these companies include, but certainly are not limited to, Brookes Publishing, Research Press, and Woodbine House. It might be worth your while to get a copy of their catalogs or check out their websites.

You might have noticed that many of the books I've mentioned were first published quite a while ago. Well, the laws of learning haven't changed and since these books are still readily available after all this time, that speaks pretty well to their usefulness and popularity. Enjoy your reading, and may you be greatly reinforced when you use ABA!

REFERENCES

Ayllon, T. and Azrin, N. (1968) *The Token Economy*. Englewood Cliffs, NJ: Prentice-Hall.

Baker, B. L., Brightman, A. J., Blacher, J. B., Heifitz, L .J. *et al.* (2004) *Steps to Independence*. Baltimore, MD: Brookes Publishing.

Bandura, A. (ed.) (1974) *Psychological Modeling: Conflicting Theories*. New York, NY: Lieber-Atherton.

Becker, W. C. (1971) *Parents are Teachers*. Champaign, IL: Research Press.

Bijou, S. (1995) *Behavior Analysis of Child Development*. Reno, NV: Context Press.

Cautela, J. R., Cautela, J. and Esonis, S. (1983) *Forms for Behavior Analysis with Children*. Champaign, IL: Research Press.

Cautela, J. R., and Groden, J. (1978) *Relaxation: A Comprehensive Manual for Adults, Children and Children with Special Needs*. Champaign, IL: Research Press.

Cautela, J. R. and Ishaq, W. (eds) (1996) *Contemporary Issues in Behavior Therapy: Improving the Human Condition*. New York, NY: Plenum Press.

Cautela, J. R. and Kearney, A. J. (1986) *The Covert Conditioning Handbook*. New York, NY: Springer.

Cautela, J. R. and Kearney, A. J. (1990) "Overview of Behavioral Treatment." In M. E. Thase, B. A. Edelstein and M. Hersen (eds) *Handbook of Outpatient Treatment of Adults*. New York, NY: Plenum Press.

Cooper, J., Heron, T.E. and Heward, W.L. (2007) *Applied Behavior Analysis* (second edition). Upper Saddle River, NJ: Prentice-Hall.

Glasberg, B. A. (2005) *Functional Behavior Assessment for People with Autism*. Bethesda, MD: Woodbine House.

Goldstein, A. P., Sprafkin, R. P. and Gershaw, N. J. (1976) *Skill Training for Community Living: Applying Structured Learning Therapy*. New York, NY: Pergamon.

Gray, C. and White, A. L. (eds) (2002) *My Social Stories Book*. London: Jessica Kingsley Publishers.

Groden, G. (1993) "Treatment of Inappropriate Emotional Responding to Criticism by a Young Man with Autism Using Covert Conditioning." In J. R. Cautela and A. J. Kearney (eds) *Covert Conditioning Casebook*. Pacific Grove, CA: Brooks/Cole.

Kazdin, A. (1977) *The Token Economy*. New York, NY: Plenum.

Keenan, M., Kerr, K. P. and Dillenburger, K. (eds) (1999) *Parents' Education as Autism Therapists: Applied Behavior Analysis in Context*. London: Jessica Kingsley Publishers.

Krumboltz, J. D. and Krumboltz, H. B. (1972) *Changing Children's Behavior*. Englewood Cliffs, NJ: Prentice-Hall.

Nikopoulos, C. and Keenan, M. (2006) *Video Modeling and Behavior Analysis*. London: Jessica Kingsley Publishers.

Patterson, G. R. (1976) *Living with Children*. Champaign, IL: Research Press.

Reynolds, G. S. (1968) *A Primer of Operant Conditioning.* Glenview, IL: Scott Foresman.

Sidman, M. (1989) *Coercion and its Fallout.* Boston, MA: Authors Cooperative.

Skinner, B. F. (1957) *Verbal Behavior.* New York, NY: Appleton-Century-Crofts.

Skinner, B. F. (1968) *The Technology of Teaching.* New York, NY: Appleton-Century-Crofts.

Stocking, S. H., Arezzo, D. and Leavitt, S. (1979) *Helping Kids Make Friends.* Allen, TX: Argus Communications.

Sulzer, B. and Mayer, G. R. (1972) *Behavior Modification Procedures for School Personnel.* Hinsdale, IL: Dryden Press.

Tharpe, R. G. and Wetzel, R. J. (1969) *Behavior Modification in the Natural Environment.* New York, NY: Academic Press.

Ullman, L. P. and Krasner, L. (eds) (1965) *Case Studies in Behavior Modification.* New York, NY: Holt, Rinehart and Winston.

Wolpe, J. (1958) *Psychotherapy by Reciprocal Inhibition.* Stanford, CA: Stanford University Press.

Wolpe, J. and Wolpe, D. (1988) *Life Without Fear.* Oakland, CA: New Harbinger.

SUBJECT INDEX

AUTHOR INDEX

Arezzo, D. 107
Ayllon, T. 108
Azrin, N. 108

Baker, B.L. 107
Bandura, A. 53
Becker, W.C. 107
Bijou, S. 107

Cautela, J. 68
Cautela, J.R. 61, 68, 94, 105
Cooper, J. 109

Esonis, S. 68

Gershaw, N.J. 92
Glasberg, B.A. 108
Goldstein, A.P. 92
Gray, C. 93
Groden, G. 56, 94

Ishaq, W. 105

Kazdin, A. 108
Keenan, M. 93, 108
Krasner, L. 20
Krumboltz, H.B. 107
Krumboltz, J.D. 107

Leavitt, S. 107

Mayer, G.R. 31, 108

Nikopoulos, C. 93

Patterson, G.R. 98, 107

Reynolds, G.S. 36

Sidman, M. 46, 108
Skinner, B.F. 20—1, 29
Sprafkin, R.P. 92

Stocking, S.H. 107
Sulzer, B. 31, 108

Tharpe, R.G. 108

Ullman, L.P. 20

Wetzel, R.J. 108
White, A.L. 93
Wolpe, D. 55
Wolpe, J. 22, 55